MOSAIC
ART TODAY

MOSAIC
ART TODAY

LARRY ARGIRO

State University College of Education
New Paltz, New York

INTERNATIONAL TEXTBOOK COMPANY
Scranton, Pennsylvania

INTERNATIONAL TEXTBOOKS IN ART EDUCATION
Italo L. de Francesco, Consulting Editor

To My Wife Lucy
and Son Aldo

Foreword

If there is any truth in the statement "Those who can't do, teach; and those who can't teach, teach others how to teach," it certainly is not true of the author, Larry Argiro. At once a fine craftsman and an excellent teacher, he is eminently qualified to write about an area in which he is both an accomplished practitioner and a fine teacher of teachers. A professional mosaic artist, who has had a wide range of activity, from the designing and installation of large mosaic murals in schools and other public buildings to the production of mosaic objects for the home, he brings to his classes at the State University College of Education, New Paltz, New York, a wealth of practical experience and a lifetime of interest and study in the art. It is this dual-experience as a designer-craftsman and as a teacher of the craft that equips him so well to write this book, for being expert in a craft and at the same time able to communicate and transfer one's knowledge and experience to others are quite different and distinct accomplishments.

We shall not attempt to emulate those writers of forewords to books who seek to summarize in a few prosaic lines what the author has to say on a subject about which they usually know far less than the author. We shall leave it to the author to explain the phenomena whereby an ancient art has been re-born as a contemporary medium for expression, well-suited to the idiom of today. We shall let him tell us why there is a continually increasing interest in mosaic art on the part of artists and craftsmen, and why this art is increasing in popularity with educators and students. We have a feeling that, in addition to the thrill of the materials and the process of using them, there is something unique about this medium that appeals to the creative capacities of the artist, designer, and student. Perhaps it is because it lends itself so well to the intuitive designer and experimenter who, freed from the rules and prototypes of yesterday's art, can arrange and re-arrange mosaic tesserae to his heart's content until he is contented with the result.

In offering to share his experience and knowledge of the craft with others, the author-craftsman becomes the artist-teacher. Well known for his educational contributions, including numerous lectures and demonstrations on mosaic art, Larry Argiro is a past president of the New York State Art Teachers Association. He has contributed many articles on mosaics and other areas of art to various periodicals. Speaking from the vantage point of the artist as well as the educator, his book should find ready acceptance among designer-craftsmen as well as teachers and students of art, industrial arts, and other areas of design. Eschewing the snares of the gimmick-maker which so often profane a fine craft by reducing it to a few tricks, patterns, and formulas, the author presents mosaic art as a medium for creative contemporary expression, well grounded in the traditions of time. In illustrating the original, inventive productions of others, past and present, he seeks to stimulate others to be likewise creative.

D. KENNETH WINEBRENNER
Editor
School Arts Magazine

Editor's Preface

The title of this book, *Mosaic Art Today*, is more than an assembly of articles and illustrations on the subject. It is a continuity in a revival of an old art practiced by ancient cultures, notably the Romans and later the Byzantines. In this respect, this volume replaces, in the mainstream of art, a mode of expression which, at one time, had assumed full stature as a decorative form; actually, it replaced painting during certain periods in art history.

The revival is relatively recent. But its inherent vitality, the naturalness of the media it employs, and the flexibility of its uses in modern life have made a definite impact upon our time. This impact derives not so much from newness as it does from the creative potential of the art itself. Self-expression, through mosaic, seems as natural as working with crayon, paint, or other media. In fact the tactile qualities of the materials add the pleasure of manipulation to an otherwise satisfying way of creating design.

The author is not a novice in this art. He has studied and experimented, has produced for self-satisfaction as well as for legitimate gain, in this old medium. He has had ample opportunity to see what children and young people can do with mosaics, and now shares with co-workers in art education what he has discovered and what he hopes others will want to experience.

The writing of the material is educationally sound and logical in its presentation. The illustrations are not only evidences of what can be accomplished but examples of good craftsmanship.

Finally, how can this book be used to best advantage? It is not a book with illustrations to be imitated, or one to be followed as "the law." The good teacher will use it as a source of information and inspiration, as a springboard from which to take off on one's own adventure in the designing of mosaics.

I. L. DE FRANCESCO
Consulting Editor

Preface

During the past five years, a revival of mosaics has emerged throughout the Western Hemisphere with startling success. While in many parts of Europe many mosaic studios continue the production of religious panels in a stereotyped traditional style, artists in America have created, in recent years, mosaics which are truly fresh and exciting. These contemporary mosaics have found a place in museums, on the façades of buildings, and in homes.

This book was written at the suggestion of many people everywhere who became interested in mosaics and wished to learn more about them. The first part of the book is devoted to a brief summary of the art of mosaics during past civilizations. An attempt was made to trace the development of this art and to point out some of the more important monuments.

The illustrations in this part were selected to help the reader gain an insight into the various styles of mosaics. Included are illustrations of early mosaic floors made during the beginning of the Roman Empire and later by some Renaissance artists. Similarly shown are the more intimate portraits and figure studies from Roman villas of the past and the magnificent murals which depicted and extolled the Christian story.

Another consideration in the choice of illustrations was a desire to point out the range of materials and techniques that were used. This is made clear when one compares the mosaics of the fish, symbol of Christianity, as found at Porec, and the jewel-like portrait of a Roman girl made of very small pieces of marble and ground to a fine finish.

The primary emphasis of the book is on the principal areas of the development of modern mosaics. A departure from the past in the transformation of mosaics into a medium for strong artistic expression is seen by the works of nationally known mosaicists who have given new directions and meaning to the problem of religious, architectural, and interior design.

The long awaited reunion of mosaic and architecture is shown and commented upon. Examples of architectural murals which were designed and executed by recognized artists show the challenges and possibilities that lie ahead.

The new conversion and application of mosaics for uses in the home are given extensive attention and coverage. Two reasons motivated this effort. First, the numerous ways in which mosaics can help make the modern home more attractive and serviceable. Second, the suggestion is made that most people, irrespective of art training and experience, could enrich their homes and their lives by working with mosaics.

Although this book was not written purely as a text, the many illustrations of mosaics made by students of various abilities and training and the technical procedures which are described should help guide those persons of any age level toward satisfactory solution of their own attempts at designing mosaics. There are no patterns to follow or designs to copy here. Works created by students and professionals using many approaches and materials were included to show the results achieved by those approaching mosaic making with a fresh viewpoint and an experimental attitude.

The sections dealing with materials, tools, and processes were placed toward the end of the book. It was planned in this manner. It is believed that anyone wishing to work in mosaics would first want to know some-thing about them—what mosaics really are, where were these developed, the potential and limitation of the medium.

This sense of history, understanding, and appreciation of mosaics will be the crucial role and synthesis—the necessary link—to satisfactory and successful work in mosaics, and will add the special stimulus to original work and a total asthetic experience.

LARRY ARGIRO
State University College of Education
New Paltz, New York

Acknowledgments

Thanks to my brother Nicholas for his interest and enthusiasm for mosaics, which in turn sustained my own; to his wife Patricia for reading parts of the manuscript and making valuable suggestions; to Florence Baisler for typing some chapters; to Roger Lintault, Leo Irrera, and Neil Croom for their early encouragement and help in photography; to Bernard Barnes and Mohamad Towfique for making several transparencies and other photographs; to the many students who gave form to my suggestions and teaching and especially Stephen Goldberg for photographing several works; to John Bodor for spending many hours in the dark room; and to Stephen Feldman for his drawings of some details.

Special thanks to Elsa Schmid for her views and warmth; to D. Kenneth Winebrenner for his confidence; to Italo L. de Francesco for his faith; to Kenneth R. Gromlich for supervising the publication of the book with personal care; to Robert Ross for his design of the book and the book jacket; and to the International Textbook Company for the courtesies extended.

And my thanks to the many mosaicists, schools, studios, and publications who contributed photographs and who are identified in the legends accompanying each illustration.

L. A.

Contents

MOSAIC
ART TODAY

INTRODUCTION

From Ancient Splendor . . .

A true art form never really becomes obsolete. It enjoys periods of fabulous popularity, it may be neglected for some time, but eventually it will emerge again and again as a potent force in the endeavor of creative people. An outstanding example of this is the current revival of interest in mosaic art—one of the oldest art forms—which had its beginning over 5000 years ago in Egypt and reached its pinnacle during the Byzantine Empire and again in the early Christian era in Italy.

The art of mosaic—the same glowing art that covered the floors of Pompeii and bejeweled the walls of Ravenna, Santa Sofia, and countless other great cathedrals—has again become one of the most exciting means for aesthetic expression for the modern artist.

Many of our contemporary artists and craftsmen have attempted, with striking success, to help revive this unusual art. Some of these modern artists made visits to the shrines and cathedrals in Palermo, Rome, Monreale, Constantinople, Ravenna, and others where they could breathe still the pious beauty and splendor of mosaic art in all its glory.

They were intrigued and impressed by the sparkling splendor of S. Apollinare Nuovo, Galla Placidia, and the Justinian and Theodora murals, and by the rich and glowing gold in Venice and Ravenna; they marveled at the changes in tone which seemed to give life to each area of color; they saw the irregular, hand-cut tesserae which gave surfaces a surprising vitality and flooded space with reflected light; they were inspired by the simple, almost modern, designs which respect the characteristic flatness of the wall; and they observed the cementing of each small cube of enamel in a directional manner, following one another around outlines of shapes, thus giving movement and animation to the designs themselves.

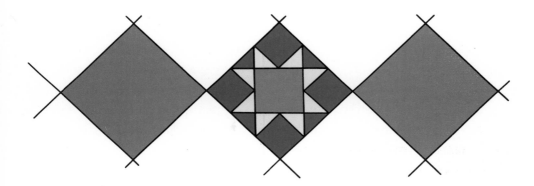

Green marble mosaic design. Pisa Cathedral.

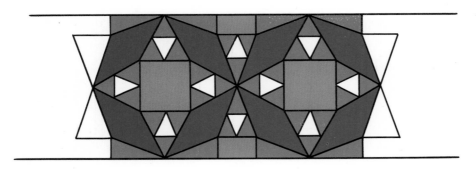

Design of a colored mosaic made of marble. Santa Maria Maggiore, Tivoli.

3

. . . To Modern Excitement

One wonders why it took so long for the modern artist to rediscover mosaics. This is especially significant with the realization that the post-Cezanne period in painting eliminated space in favor of organized planes and color, for mosaic is essentially active color in organized planes.

The vitality and force of the current revival in mosaic art has had a telling impact on artists, architects, furniture designers, decorators, and art educators. Rarely has a movement in art been so quick to awaken our creative efforts toward so many possibilities.

Mosaic art makes it possible to transform bits and chunks of glass, enamel, ceramic tiles, pebbles, shells, and many other hard and interesting materials into delightful, rich, patterned surfaces as colorful and translucent as a patchwork of gems — and much more lasting. It is an excellent medium for serious creative expression, designing wall plaques and murals of unusual brilliancy and movement, especially when using the sparkling "smalti," the small cubes of hand-cut glass or enamel. It is well recognized that a picture created with mosaics frequently emanates more vitality and strength than most other media.

The designer, aware of the durability of mosaic, has brought it into the home with startling success. It seems to function efficiently indoors as a coffee-table top, a table-lamp base, or a decorative panel, and outdoors as a facing for a pool, a garden decoration, or a terrace table. Drama and poetry, color and brilliancy, are combined in mosaic to bring distinction and beauty to a home. Years of service are also a charactertistic of mosaic. The practical-minded craftsman and hobbyist will see the advantages of this vitreous-stone-and-cement process as an excellent craft for the making of lasting, impervious surfaces — spot and scratch proof.

Mosaic panel of colored glass and ceramic tile in cement backing, by the author.

To New Adventures . . .

Before definite suggestions are made for the introduction of mosaic in the classroom, it is imperative to discuss some possible implications from an educational point of view.

We are aware of the practice, too often observed in some of our schools, of making a fetish or a fad of new ideas and processes. We seem to go "wild" or "all out" for anything which is new or novel merely for the sake of the newness or novelty of it alone—the making of things—rather than for what educative elements there may be in a particularly new activity.

Mosaic art offers immense possibilities for the creative growth of our youth when taught with experimental sensitivity and insight. The opportunity to handle each small chunk of hard and colorful material, to move it about, thus making decisions and choices as to shape, size, color, texture, reflective quality, and directional movement, promotes the aesthetic development of the participant. The very nature of the material used in making mosaics should be a springboard to bold and imaginative work and the creation of exciting new designs.

To be sure, making mosaics can be a very fascinating process. But we mustn't allow this factor to become the primary concern. The discoveries which the student makes while working with mosaic materials should be uppermost in the mind of the teacher.

The student should discover that mosaics function best when conceived as flat areas — respecting the quality of the material on hand — rather than attempting illusions of depth or poor imitations of the natural. The discovery that a mosaic object should be appreciated for its own intrinsic value, the adherence to the truthfulness of the material in developing a design-idea as a spatial problem rather than the accurate description of a real object, will help the student understand the aspirations, problems, and concepts which preoccupy the contemporary artist, and at the same time gain an insight of the art problem throughout the ages.

This approach does not negate or diminish the importance of the product. For too many years now we have observed the delight which the successful completion of a particular object or art problem generates in an individual. A child, especially, grows in self-realization when the art activity is properly balanced by a sound process-product concept.

Yes, the product is important, but so is the process. For if the process is sincere and wholesome, and it has helped develop the participant creatively, then the product will be good and also unique — thus giving a true sense of personal accomplishment so important to every individual in a world whose future may be drastically altered by oncoming automation.

II PAST GLORIES OF MOSAIC ART

The Mystery of the Ages

The art of mosaics seems shrouded in the mystery of the ages. The literature on the subject is rather meager and we observe some differences as to its origin. "The earliest existing specimens of mosaic belong to one of the less important branches of the art—namely, the ornamentation on a small scale of jewelry, ivory thrones, and other furniture" according to *The Encyclopedia Britannica*, 11th edition. A more glamorous point of view is taken by Charles H. Sherrill in *Mosaics*. He says, "Mosaic was really rather a snob. It frankly chose to install itself near the seats of the mighty—critics may even call it a little brother of the rich. It preferred great capitals of empires like Rome, Constantinople. . . . Thanks, then, to mosaic's snobbishness, it will be the world's high spots in the days when the Mediterranean was the world. . . ."

Be that as it may, it is conceded that mosaic art had its beginning as a floor decoration. Flat stones and pieces of marble were used to cover floors in the same manner as we today cover our floors with cork, linoleum, or asphalt. Before we get too involved with techniques and processes, it may be interesting to take a look at the persons who made mosaics. These craftsmen were called *imaginarius*, a happy connotation relating that the early mosaicists were designers with imagination, much like the feeling of the contemporary mosaicist. During these early days, his ability as a designer and his skill was highly regarded, since he was the highest paid of all the men employed. Emperor Diocletian proclaimed in an edict that the imaginarius received 175 sesterces per day, while other artists and craftsmen ranged down from 75 for a pictor parietarius to 50 for a lapidarius structor, a calcis coctor, or a musearius.

Fragment of a mosaic floor represent-ing a fish—symbol of early Christian faith. Porec, 4th century. (Yugoslovia Information Office.)

The implications of this worthy recognition is readily understood when standing in front of an early 8th-century mosaic covering the entire wall of a Damascus mosque's courtyard. The subtle use of imagination is here too evident and vital, since the imaginarius has invested simple objects such as houses, trees, rivers, and brooks with life and meaning in the face of iconoclastic dogmas.

Detail from Roman floor. Museo Nazionale, Naples.

Emperor Justinian, his crowned head ringed by a halo, holds plate with Eucharistic bread to symbolize his priestly role. San Vitale, Ravenna, 6th century.

Classifications of Mosaics

These following simple classifications of mosaic are given by Gauckler in *Dictionnaire des Antiquites*:

Opus tesselatum, consisting of cubes of marble or stone, regularly disposed in simple patterns. This type of mosaic work was largely used for pavements, especially in Roman times.

Opus vermiculatum, consisting of cubes, irregularly shaped, generally of colored marble or more precious materials, when these were obtainable, disposed so as to obtain a pictorial effect. The "art" of mosaic is mainly concerned with this type of work.

Opus musivum, properly applied to the mosaic decoration of walls and vaulted ceilings in which cubes of glass or enamel were used. The glass was rendered opaque by the addition of oxide of tin, and colored with other metallic oxides; when melted, it was cast into small slabs. generally about one-half inch thick. and then broken into small cubes.

Type of Cosmati mosaic found around spiral columns. Orvieto Cathedral.

Pattern of a Cosmati mosaic. San Lorenzo, Rome.

Opus sectile, a species of marqueterie in marble or other colored materials used to produce pictures and patterns. Under a later empire, a particular variety of this type of work called "opus alexandrinum," mainly composed of red and green porphyry, was much in use.

Cosmati, a type of decoration used on columns where the marble base is used as a matrix in which spaces are chiseled out to receive and hold glass tesserae. At times, flutings were suggested by parallel bands of tesserae on straight columns; twisted columns are often decorated with spiral bands of gold and colored enamel cubes. This style was mainly employed by the Cosmati family in Italy from the 6th to the 14th century. Fine examples are found in many cities of northern Italy and in Rome, Monreale, and in the Taj Mahal at Agra.

Illustration of a detail of "opus sectile" as found in the Monreale Cathedral. Oriental influence is observed. 12th century.

Twisted columns decorated with Cosmati mosaics. Church of Ara Coeli, Rome.

*Cosmati mosaic columns in cloisters
of Monreale Cathedral. 12th century.
(Italian Tourist Office.)*

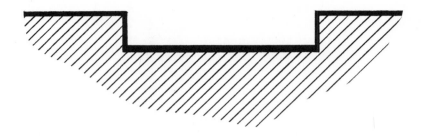

Cross section showing the area chiseled out of a marble surface to fit enamel tesserae.

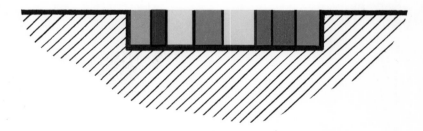

Cross section showing the enamel tesserae set in place in the process of making a Cosmati mosaic.

Portrait of young girl. Roman mosaic, Museo Nazionale, Naples.

Roman Mosaics

Roman pavements were usually made of pieces of marble from one-half to one-quarter of an inch square, but irregular in shape. A few very unusual kinds of mosaic floors, such as the Isola Farnese (near Rome), were found to be made of small tiles of green glass. In the case of the *House of the Faun*, at Pompeii, greater brilliance was achieved when small quantities of glass tesserae were imbedded among the marble ones.

Mosaic craftsman restoring parts of a Roman mosaic floor at Piazza Armerina. Similar scenes were a familiar sight 1600 years ago as mosaicists from Africa were building Maximian's villa in Sicily.

Captured bird being carried on gang-
way by one of Emperor Maximian's
guards. Mosaic was made of marble
tesserae. Corridor of the Great Hunting Scene, Piazza Armerina, 2nd
century.

The early imaginarius, or mosaicist, of the pre-Christian era devoted his talents almost entirely to the designing and execution of floor mosaics. These earlier mosaics, some of which were seen recently at Agrigento, were made of geometric patterns of squares, stars, and interlacing ribbonlike shapes. Other fine examples of these are to be found all around the Mediterranean, including some in France, Germany, and England and in Africa.

A recent archeological discovery at Piazza Armerina in Sicily gives new insights of the highly developed art of floor mosaics. This summer residence, believed to have been built by a Roman general around A.D. 280, contains over 38,000 square feet of mosaic floors made with small cubes of varicolored marble.

Hunting scenes, the capture of wild animals, and the transport of the beast dominate the large floors. The most unusual floor, generally very popular with tourists, is the *Chamber of the Ten Maidens*. Ten young women are shown in very succinct dress consisting of the *subligaria*, very short bathing slip and narrow brassiere, much like the modern "bikini." Expert opinion agrees that this scene represents a Roman aquatic competition.

Close observation of these mosaic floors reveal a strong African influence. It is thought that African craftsmen, familiar with the details of hippopotamuses, lions, tigers, and similar animals, were brought to Piazza Armerina to work for the Roman general.

Although few wall mosaics were found in Pompeii, a most sensitive portrait of a girl from this period is now in the National Museum of Naples. However, in a sense, these ancient wall mosaics were considered in the same class as floor mosaics, installed out in the open because of their endurance and imperviousness to the weather. Thus far, mosaics were primarily used because of their durability. Eventually mosaics leave the floor and find their rightful place on the walls of the fabulous cathedrals of Istanbul, Monreale, and Ravenna.

A European trip would be incomplete without a visit to Piazza Armerina in the south of Italy and to Ravenna to the north. A new road now makes Piazza Armerina very accessible and a fine hotel has just been completed in that city.

Mosaic floor of the Chamber of the Ten Maidens. Piazza Armerina, 2nd century.

From Floors to Walls

The development from floors to walls — this change from pure utility to religious meaning — is credited to the early Christians, according to Sherrill. He says: "Let us be fair to the early Christians, and credit them with the launching of a new craft. Their beginnings in wall mosaics were, of course, confined to such secret places as catacombs, since their new religion was rigorously proscribed. Because those obscure haunts of theirs were badly lighted, if lighted at all, Christian symbolism expressed itself on catacomb walls, and not on the even darker floors. There are preserved in Rome over a dozen examples of these early mural efforts, crude, if you will, but ancestors of a noble craft. Then suddenly this Christian symbolism was granted freedom to emerge into the light of day."

The conversion of Emperor Constantine to the new religion gave new impetus and drive to the followers of Christ and new meaning to the symbols of the new faith. Emerging from the darkness of the catacombs into the freedom of the sunlight, mosaic art now found its rightful place on the imposing walls and ceilings of the new houses of worship. The new art assumed a profound scope for the spread of Christianity and its symbolism. And because of the new challenge, the imaginarius developed new techniques and materials with which to adorn the new basilicas and sing the glories of the new religion.

Byzantine Mosaics

The tomb of Galla Placidia in Ravenna is the most striking example of the effective fusion of mosaics and architecture. Here, the mosaic becomes an integral part of the mausoleum and in doing so, it creates an unearthly feeling, a sensation of subtle calm and deep meditation.

The tomb, built about A.D. 440, is more like a small church in the form of a cross. One enters the tomb in semidarkness, for this is the only way to discover and enjoy the delightful and gentle harmony and the dignity of style of these mosaics which words cannot describe — and shouldn't.

The entire theme of the interior of the tomb is a play of multiblue tesserae and touches of gold and mother-of-pearl which add a subdued sparkle, unlike the later mosaics in which gold was too lavishly used.

A striking example of Byzantine mosaic. Detail of Adam and Eve found in island of Chios, 11th century. Rediscovered by Skira's Asia Minor expedition. (Skira Books.)

*Interior of Tomb of Galla Placidia,
Ravenna. Panes of one-half inch alabaster allow just the right amount of
light for viewing the mosaic. 5th
century. (Italian Tourist Office.)*

A Chronological Selection of Some of the Most Important Glass
Wall-mosaics

4th CENTURY

Rome	Santa Costanza
	Santa Maria Maggiore
	Santa Pudenziana
	San Giovanni in Laterano
Naples	Santa Restituta
Milan	San Lorenzo
Porec	Euphrasius' Basilica, floor

5th CENTURY

Ravenna	Orthodox Baptistery
	Galla Placidia
	Archbishop's Chapel
Naples	San Giovanni in Fonte
Rome	San Paolo fuori le mura
	Santa Maria Maggiore
	Santa Sabina
Milan	Sant' Ambrogio
Fundt	Cathedral
Nola	Cathedral
San Prisco	Santa Matrona

Emperor Justinian, detail of
page 11. San Vitale, Raven
century. (Skira Books.)

6th CENTURY

Ravenna	Arian Baptistery
	San Apollinare Nuovo
	San Vitale
	San Apollinare in Classe
Rome	Santi Cosmas and Damian
Istanbul	Santa Sofia
Thessalonica	San George
	Santa Sofia
Trebizond	Santa Sofia
Porec	Euphrasius' Basilica, apse

7th CENTURY

Rome	Santa Agnese fuori le mura
	San Teodoro
	Santo Stefano
	San Venanzio
Jerusalem	Dome of the Rock

8th CENTURY

Rome	Baptistery, San Giovanni in Laterano
	Santi Nereus and Achilles
Jerusalem	Mosque of Al-Aksa
Mount Sinai	Chapel of Transfiguration

9th CENTURY

Rome	Santa Cecilia in Trastevere
	San Marco
	Santa Maria della Navicella
	San Prassede
Milan	San Ambrogio

10th CENTURY

Cordova	Mihrab Mosque

11th CENTURY

Jerusalem	Dome of the Rock, base of cupola
Istanbul	Church of San Saviour, walls and domes

Detail from Noah's Ark. St. Mark,
Venice, 12th century.

12th CENTURY

Venice	San Marco, narthex, apse and walls
Daphne	Daphne Church, narthex
Capua	Cathedral, apse
Torcello	Cathedral, apse, walls
Murano	Cathedral, apse
Salerno	Cathedral, apse
Palermo	Cappella Palatina, all walls
	La Martorana Church, vault
Monreale	Cathedral, all walls
Bethlehem	Church of the Nativity
Cefalu'	Cathedral, apse
Rome	San Clemente, apse
	Santa Francesca Romana, apse
	Santa Maria in Trastevere, apse

13th CENTURY

Florence	Baptistery, vault
	San Miniato, apse and west front
	San Paolo fuori le mura, apse
	San Clemente, arch
	San Giovanni in Laterano, apse
	Santa Maria Maggiore, apse and west end
	Santa Maria in Trastevere, apse

14th CENTURY

Florence	Baptistery
Pisa	Cathedral, east apse
Rome	San Peter, navicella
	Santa Maria in Cosmedin, walls
Venice	Santi Giovanni a Paolo, arch

Dream of St. Thomas. St. Mark,
Venice, 12th century.

33

*Exterior of Monreale Cathedral highly
decorated with glass and gold mosaics.
12th century. (Italian Tourist Office.)*

III MOSAIC AS EXPRESSION

The art of mosaic has enjoyed a new popularity in recent years. This revival of interest is purely an American affair.

Mosaicists in Europe and elsewhere have been continuously busy, to be sure. Mosaic studios in Venice, Ravenna, and New York have produced murals, usually in a religious vein, for many years. Murals of this type are designed in sketch form, then translated by craftsmen into mosaic murals. Mosaic work of this nature cannot be called expressive in the strictest sense of the word.

This is not a discussion in aesthetics or art criticism, but mention must be made of the practice which produces works of art, "long distance," in the field of mosaics.

JESUS AND MARY *a moving and dramatic interpretation by Louisa Jenkins.*

Wall design by P. D. Halloman. Glazed ceramic tesserae and hand-etched glazed tile inset. (Mosaic Crafts, New York.)

THE BIRDS, *by John Kidder and James Dorris. Smalti tesserae by indirect method, polished brass edging 54 x 24 inches. (Mosaic Crafts, New York.)*

Watching mosaic artisans transform a water color sketch into a full size mosaic mural, one wonders about the feeling, freshness, and spontaneity of the original design idea. Forceful, creative expression in mosaic requires personal involvement with materials. The kinesthetic and tactile experience of selecting one tessera and rejecting another, and the physical act in setting it in place, watching it contribute and develop a sensation of spatial and surface animation are essential.

It is doubted that the effects of reflected light, rhythmic directional movement, intensity of color, and unusual textures — elements which a good mosaic possesses — can be expressed via a color sketch and interpreted by an artisan thousands of miles distant . . . or next door.

It must be conceded, however, that when the nature of a mural is purely decorative and consisting of large areas of color, the practice of "farming out" its execution has certain legitimacy and advantages. This is particularly true in the case of the designer who knows and understands the true nature of the mosaics and who may, in person, supervise and watch the execution of the mosaic mural and thus make changes as the work develops.

Several mosaic artists in America have infused new life in this very old medium through the introduction of special techniques. These workers in the arts, expressing feelings and ideas in old and new materials, breaking frontiers with new concepts, have restored mosaic to the eminent position it once held.

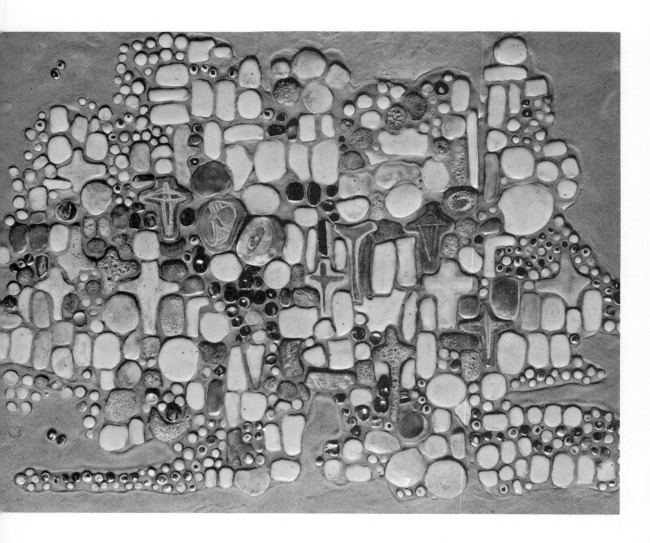

WHITE ON WHITE, by Frances E. Simches. Ceramic on concrete, 28 x 36 inches. (American Craftsmen's Council, New York.)

BLUE GARDEN, *by Ros Barron. Ceramic tile on concrete, 23 x 26 inches. (American Craftsmen's Council, New York.)*

Mosaicist Jeanne Reynal made a strong case for individualism recently when she wrote in *It Is*, "In the art of mosaic, tactile values take precedence over painterly values; texture is all-important. To force stones to speak on painterly terms is equivalent to wringing an anecdote from oil canvas, a falsification of the medium and unpoetic. . . ." and again, ". . . today in America the emphasis in art is upon the individual adventure. But this freedom is not touched upon by craftsmen in the art of mosaic. By means of a technique available to all. permitting an immediacy of expression lost since the Renaissance, the palimpset, or third hand, is buried. I affirm that the art of mosaic can rise from the pavement where Ghirlandaio placed it. The end result must and will be judged on its quality. Mosaic to be real must be individual, coherent and luminous — the reality fresh and frightening, like every original."

The modern artists has discovered that the varicolored stones and enamels are exciting and potent means for individual expression, resulting in most striking and unusual visual statements.

UNTITLED, *by Jeanne Reynal,*
1941. Mosaic on magnesite.

THE HORNS OF MEMORY, *by Jeanne Reynal, 1954. Mosaic on magnesite cement.*

STONE PAINTING, *by Jeannie Reynal,*
1955. Mosaic on magnesite cement,
44 x 38 inches.

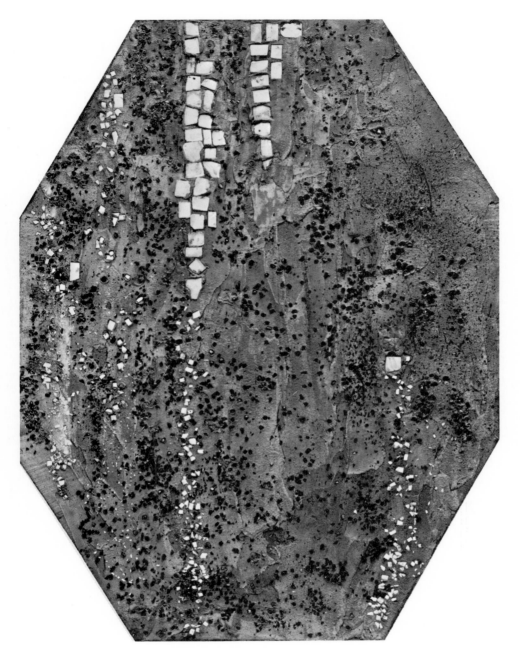

GREYING RAIN, *by Jeanne Reynal,*
1959. Mosaic on cement.

43

While working in Florence as a sculptor in 1953 and 1954, Sahl Swarz first became conscious of mosaics. He says, "Color has tempted sculptors from the beginning of time, but most of the color used has been superficial. Our own time is notable for its lack of chromatics in sculpture, mainly due to the difficulty in achieving an integrated feeling between color and form. But in mosaics the glass pieces are the form itself, instead of a nonhomogeneous, superficial embellishment. The surface, due to the hand cutting of the glass, is alive; it vibrates with diverse reflections at all angles. Color areas can be naturally modified for complementary relationships by the mixing of colors to take advantage of the pointillistic effect of the medium. In other words, the colors are not solid; they are made up of endless fragments with cement between, so that their spacing and prominence can also be varied. This adds up to an unusual opportunity for plastic manipulation. . . . The little I have done in the medium of mosaic sculpture assures me that this new approach to an ancient art form as a brilliant future. . . . Visualize how much more inviting and colorful our public places will be when decorated with mosaics in the round!"

HEAD OF CHRIST, by *Sahl Swarz,
1954. Steel and mosaic, 30 inches
high. Base of travertine marble,
letters carved in intaglio and filled
with tesserae, head built as in
"Ox." (Sculpture Center, New
York.)*

KAFKA, by Sahl Swarz, 1953. Steel and mosaic, 33 inches high. Hair and neck are rust-colored steel. Smalti tesserae of varying shades of green cemented on sculpture. (Sculpture Center, New York.)

Ox, by Sahl Swarz, 1953. Steel and
mosaic, 27 inches long. Figure of the
ox built of welded steel, allowing for
thickness of cement and glass mosaic.
Steel rod seen on the surface is welded
to the base metal form, and serves to
mark change of plane, color, or for
linear accent. (Sculpture Center, New
York.)

Serious experimental work in mosaics during the last decade has taken place in the studios of Elsa Schmid, Jeanne Reynal, Max Spivak, A. de Bethune, Sahl Swarz, Margot and Jack Stewart, and others in the East. Also, Louisa Jenkins, Juan O'Gorman, Robert Mallary, Mary Bowling, and others in California.

An unusual approach for an outdoor mural combining mosaic, relief forms, and iron, designed and executed by Louisa Jenkins for The College of Holy Names in California. Oro tesserae is profusely used.

Center panel of a triptych by Louisa Jenkins, who uses lava rock, iridescent furnace slag, crystal, mica, and the traditional smalti to produce extraordinary textural and color effects in her mosaics.

Mosaic sculpture made with field stones and small tesserae. Epoxy type glue was used.

GIRL PLAYING A FLUTE *by Seff Weidl.*
A strong mosaic design made of irreg-
ular pieces of warm brown, white, and
sand-colored stones. It has been in-
stalled on the entrance wall of an apart-
ment house in Munich, Germany.
(CRAFT HORIZON.)

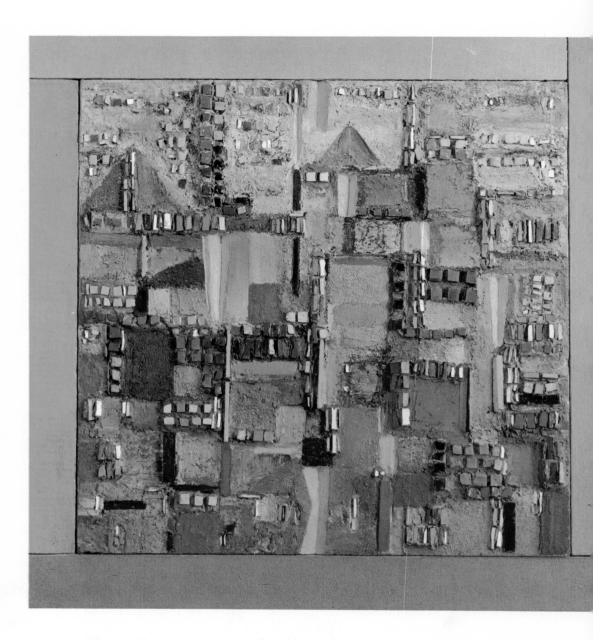

Mosaic Brussa, Evening, *by Elsa Schmid, 1958, 15¼ inch square. (Collection of Gertrude Mellon.)*

Line drawing by Elsa Schmid for the mosaic portrait FATHER D'ARCY. When compared with the finished work one observes the startling changes which took place during the development by the artist in terms of "smalti" tesserae.

FATHER D'ARCY, by Elsa Schmid, 1950. A fresco mosaic (detail). (Collection of The Museum of Modern Art, New York.)

AUSTRALIAN OPAL, by Elsa Schmid, finished in 1960. Fresco mosaic 18 x 27½ inches. Experimental work, concerned with spatial relationships, strong use of color.

Stained glass mosaic, by Jack Stewart,
1958. Transparent colored tesserae
laminated to plate glass.

WHITE RIVER, by *Margot Stewart,*
1956, 29 x 31 inches.

The work of Sister Magdalen Mary, as an artist and teacher, has been of great influence, especially among the young. Her studios at Immaculate Heart College in Los Angeles have proven to be centers of aesthetic excitement and delight for hundreds of students of all ages.

Active interest in mosaics in America is growing, and special courses are being offered at many art schools, colleges and universities. A course in mosaic is offered at State University College of Education, New Paltz, and taught by the author. Art programs throughout the country are being enriched constantly by the introduction of mosaic experiences in public schools.

GROWTH, *by the author, 1960. An abstract composition of tiny smalti sprinkled in areas flooded with thick clear lacquer. The flat shapes were made with crackled glaze sheets. The entire mosaic was sprayed with clear lacquer.*

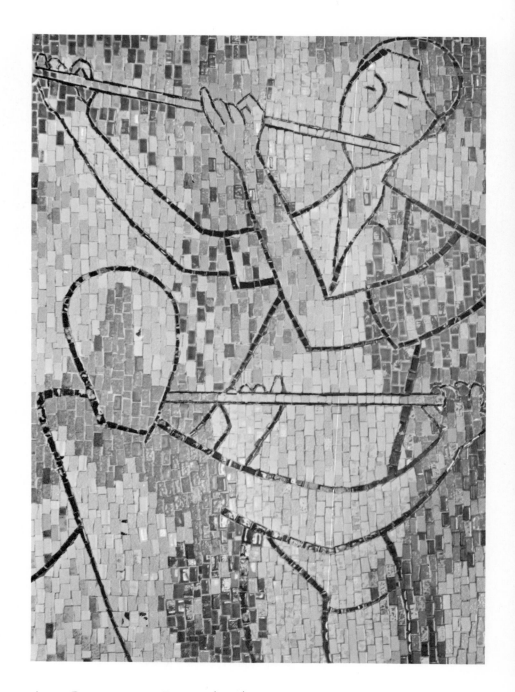

ALDO PLAYING THE FLUTE, *by the author, executed directly on Novoply backing. Ceramic tesserae, split in half, were set on thin layer of "gesso" and forming an outline of the figure in two positions on a background of fluid color areas.*

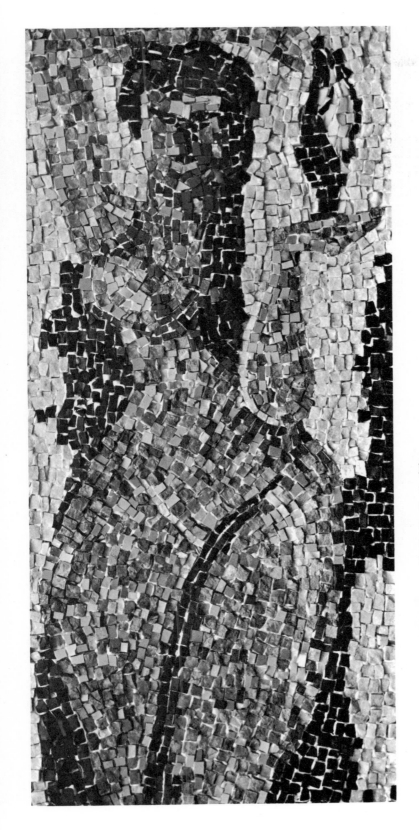

FIGURE, *by the author, which was executed directly on plywood backing by spreading a thickness of "gesso" and pressing the "marmi" tesserae, small cubes of marble, in place. The "gesso" oozes between the tesserae thus giving accent to the theme. (Collection of Dr. and Mrs. Louis J. Buchman.)*

Ecce Homo, *by the author. Smalti in* *face and shoulders, opaque glass in* *background. Direct application to ply-* *wood backing.*

SYLVIA LAKE, *by the author. Smalti tesserae directly on plywood, 36 x 48 inches. (Dr. and Mrs. John George, Verona.)*

New impetus toward restoring mosaic as an important and true art form was provided recently at the fountainhead of Byzantine mosaics — Ravenna.

Professor Giuseppe Bovini, inspector of monuments at Ravenna, in 1959 organized an exhibit of modern mosaics at the National Museum in Ravenna.

It is a thrilling experience to observe, study, and enjoy, with minor exceptions, recent mosaic creations designed by prominent painters and executed by local craftsmen in the shadow of San Vitale and Galla Placidia. One stands intrigued by the dramatic, almost palpitating and explosive panel designed and executed by Georges Mathieu and is at the next moment held speechless by the quiet dignity and unearthly splendor of Galla Placidia, only a few feet away, created by unknown imaginarius.

Plans now in progress indicate that the first Gallery of Modern Mosaics will be established at Ravenna.

The mosaic art in the Edinburgh Festival Exhibition of Byzantine Art, held in 1960 and later moved to the Victoria and Albert Museum in London, has aroused enthusiastic response in Britain. These and other strong currents suggest that the possibility of the mosaic contribution to today's art is great.

Detail of a mosaic by the young Italian, Enzo Pagani. He brings a fresh and lyrical viewpoint in the shadows of overpowering tradition. Pagani has shown successfully throughout Europe in recent years. (Galleria del Grattacielo, Legnano.)

Doves in Flight, *executed after a painting by Renato Guttuso. (National Museum, Ravenna.)*

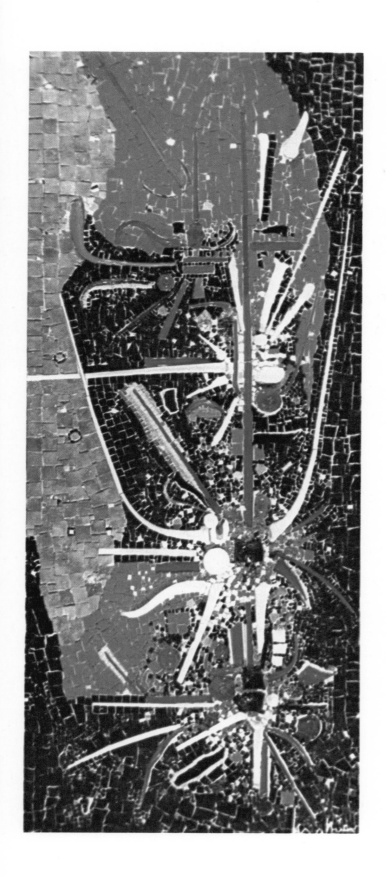

Mosaic designed and executed by French painter Georges Mathieu. Elongated masses of vitreous paste, filaments of glass, and smalti tesserae were used. (National Museum, Ravenna.)

Mosaic designed by Italian painter Corrado Cagli and executed by S. Cicognani. (Shown at the Exhibit of Modern Mosaics at National Museum, Ravenna.)

SUNBURST, *both designed and exe-cuted by Mario Deluigi, smalti tes-serae in whites with subtle underscor-ing in reds, blacks, grays, and blues. (Part of the modern mosaics shown at the National Museum at Ravenna, 1959.* CRAFT HORIZONS.*)*

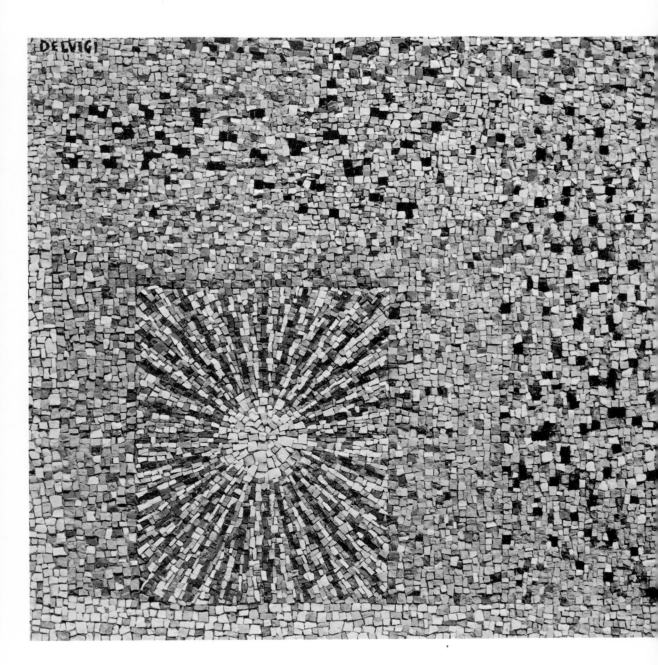

These towering mosaic structures, designed and constructed by Simon Rodia at Watts, California, fall into no strict art category. (Committee for Simon Rodia's Towers in Watts.)

Like the metal structures, Rodia's mortar forms are encrusted with broken tiles, dishes, bottles, and seashells arranged in unusual mosaic patterns.

One of the strangest creations is the mosaic structure known as Simon Rodia's Towers in Watts, California.

They are a construction of steel rods, mesh, and mortar, in a maze of forms which soar to a hundred-foot height. The weblike members are covered with a glittering incrustation of broken tiles, bottles, and seashells. Woven together by overhead arches around the spires are fountains, pavilions, and labyrinths. This walled magic garden is covered, too, with multicolored mosaic, or with imprints of tools, hands, corncobs, and baskets, interwoven here and there with the initials of their builder, a poor tile-setter who had in his mind for thirty years to do something big, to have his fingerprint on this obscure corner of the world.

One man—Simon Rodia—created the Towers without aid in 33 intensely purposeful years. He worked without plans, equipment, or scaffolding. The structures were literally "built in the air," using only the simple tools of a tile-setter, together with window-washer's belt and bucket. In gathering, Simon collected more than 70,000 seashells and countless tiles and bottles.

The Towers fall into no strict art category; they were made of discarded materials, intuitively, by an unschooled man, yet he has received unqualified response from critics the world over. It has been said that they are the greatest mosaic structure ever made by one man without aid. Critics have commented that the Towers are a unique monument to human energy, consistency, and skill; a gigantic flower of folk art. The trivial material, they point out, has lost its triviality; it has become a ligitimate medium, like the pigments and brush-strokes of the painter. From small salvaged things a crescendo of form, texture, and color have been made.

BIRD, *design by Marc Chagall and executed by mosaicist A. Rocchi. Smalti in varied range of blues. (Exhibited National Museum at Ravenna, 1959* CRAFT HORIZONS.)

MOSAICS AND ARCHITECTURE

Mosaics and architecture seem to be on the way toward a mutual rediscovery. After many years of apparent neglect on the part of architects, countless mosaic murals again add zest, color, and warmth to buildings everywhere. It is unfortunate that this recognition took long in coming.

Byzantine designers of buildings understood, with great affinity, the real purpose and function of mosaic. They realized its advantage and its true nature in permanency, as a decorative asset, and as color. They designed arches, walls, pendentives, drums, and cupolas leading and flowing into one another with continuous rhythm to receive rich and glowing mosaic murals, thus achieving perfect and satisfying unity.

The use of mosaics declined during the Middle Ages. The people of the north expressed their religious fervor through the stained glass windows, while the people of the south thrilled with wonder at the rich narrative of Giotto's frescoes.

Yet mosaics were never really forgotten. Misused as a painting medium during the Renaissance, with its concern for realism, mosaic makes a few sporadic appearances such as the decorations for the Albert Memorial and St. Paul's in England in the 19th century and later in Italy.

Mosaic mural made with Venetian glass designed by painter Eppens and executed by Mosaics. (Venecianos de Mexico, S. A., Cuernavaca, Mexico.)

Notwithstanding these efforts which seemed to lack the vigor and boldness of the Ravenna and Porec masterpieces, a revival of mosaics was still to become a reality. These were times when skilled mosaic craftsmen, in the attempt to translate design ideas of others, failed to live up to the standards set by the anonymous imaginarius of the past who was able to breathe life into tiny cubes of marble. Their eyes were very much in tune with a sense of beauty and innocence.

The commission was very clear to the author to design and execute a glass mosaic, 12 x 15 feet on portable panels to be affixed on a solid cement wall of the Nugget Casino, Sparks, Nevada. Several sketches of roosters were sent to architect Frank Green of Reno, Nevada. One was selected for the mosaic mural.

The small sketch of the rooster was enlarged on duplex paper to the actual size of mural so that it could serve as a pattern.

Full size sectional patterns of heavy
paper were cut out.

*Sectional patterns were transferred on
5-ply marine plywood and cut with a
sabre saw.*

Many modern architects, trained at the altar of pure "functionalism," brought forth great many barren façades and helped develop the so-called international style, which lacked warmth, color, and feeling, and with an absence of personality. The clinical look of most buildings erected in the 20th century, with some notable exceptions such as those by Le Corbusier, Gio Ponti, André Bloc, can be traced directly to the outburst of industrial and technological breakthroughs. A strong sense of materialism helped develop, and contribute to the misunderstanding of, the concept of "form follows function" to unfortunate extremes.

The entire outline of the rooster was covered with aluminum stripping to prevent rain-water from penetrating the wood, and the parts were assembled.

*Holes were drilled and countersunk
at strategic spots in each section.*

Venetian glass tesserae was cemented directly on plywood with a special adhesive prepared by Minnesota Mining Manufacturing Company.

Many architects were wrongly influenced by the economic revolution at the turn of the century and pressured to adopt new materials, building techniques, and mass-produced parts in order to help offset labor-economic factors. These problems were solved, for the moment, by neglecting the sense of beauty, cheerfulness, and warmth that only results when all the visual and plastic arts work together with mutual respect and affinity.

All sections were assembled for a final check. These sections were disassembled, packed, and shipped to Sparks.

Holes were drilled in the cement wall
and the sections were mounted in
place and grouted.

81

On occasions, attempts were made to bring a reconciliation of the decorative arts to architecture, but this was skin deep and negative. Covering sections of a building with a mosaic mural as an afterthought could hardly be called a compliment to either. Still, these attempts at using color again, first seen in European architecture, served to spur and encourage our own architects toward an awareness of the true character and possibilities of mosaics.

And because buildings become *public* "de facto," regardless of location and ownership, the modern painter, who retreated from so much during the last twenty years, must leave the selfishness of the "self" and show concern for the natural phenomena and the human drama. He must come to grips with the problem of communication, not in the sense of a private and personal system of shorthand symbolism for the benefit of friends and close admirers, but as a means toward the gradual modification and improvement of cultural climate for all people.

He will then become a useful and contributing member of the team of architects, community planners, designers, sculptors, painters, and craftsmen who will bring utility, distinction, and beauty to the cities of tomorrow.

At St. Joseph's Church, Victorias Milling Co., Inc., Philippines, A. de Bethune of Newport, R. I., spent several months designing and executing directly on cement walls with the help of company workman, several mosaic murals of a religious nature. Broken glass bottles, brought in by the natives, were the source of tesserae for the murals. Heavens are blue milk-of-magnesia bottles, grass is green soda bottles, and the river Jordan is "aqua" coke bottles. The artist herself embedded each piece of glass in fresh mortar. (Raymond and Rado, Architects.)

Adelaide de Bethune and Romolo Santa Ana are shown working on the mosaic on the West side. This wall, 10 x 15 feet, took about two weeks to complete, making six to eight small sections a day. An outline was made directly on cement blocks and pieces of glass and porcelain were pressed into a three-quarter inch thick layer of fresh mortar.

83

The mosaic on the East side is Christ Teaching the Doctors in the Temple *(Luke 2). Christ is seen as a teacher of teachers in this 10 x 15 feet mosaic. (St. Joseph's Church, Victorias Milling Co., Inc., Philippines.)*

In the Baptistry of St. Joseph's Church, three steps lead down to the level of the baptismal font in commemoration of the early days of Christianity when Baptism was more commonly administered by immersion. They also bring out the action of death and re-birth by walking down and rising again. On the back wall is shown the Baptism of Christ. The heavens are opening, voice of God being heard, and the Spirit of God appears as a dove at the moment when Christ emerges from the Jordan. The water of the Jordan is continued in mosaic all around the basin to indicate graphically that`a man who steps down into the waters of baptism puts on Christ. God looks upon the new Christian and says, "This is my beloved son, in whom I am well pleased." The Holy Spirit (dove) is seen as Christ rises from having been baptized by John in the Jordan. Heavens are blue milk-of-magnesia bottles, grass is green soda bottles, the Jordan is "aqua" coke bottles, the dove is pink and yellow, and the background of lettering is brown.

Various phases of Mexico's culture are shown in this immense mosaic which covers the library building at University City, Mexico. Juan O'Gorman designed and supervised these murals made of local stones in section of about three feet square. (Photo by Erma DeWitt.)

Mosaic mural designed by Mexican painter Siqueiros as part of the decorative plan of University City, Mexico.

A wall mosaic designed by the contemporary Italian mosaicist Righini. Three-quarter inch square Venetian glass was used.

Mosaic mural, of Venetian enamel, executed and set in place by V. Foscato, Inc. after a design by abstract painter Hans Hoffman. Mural can be seen in the main entrance hall of the office building at 711 Third Avenue, New York City.

A Venetian enamel mosaic mural on front of William O'Grady High School, Coney Island, New York, executed by V. Foscato, Inc. after a cartoon by painter Ben Shahn.

Mosaic mural executed by the V. Foscato, Inc. of Long Island City, New York for the Jewish Temple Beth Shalom, Union, New Jersey.

Detail of LUX ET VERITA, three-quarter inch Venetian glass was pasted face down on brown paper following the outline of the full size sketch. When finished, the mural was cut up into two to three feet irregular shapes, following the contours of the design, and transported to the site where a cement wall was prepared to receive the mural.

LUX ET VERITAS, designed and executed by the author, 4 x 30 feet, 1955. Mosaic mural of Venetian glass tesserae for the High School at Hudson Falls, New York. (Sargent, Webster, Cranshaw and Folley, Architects.)

The impact of the revival of mosaic is much too evident. It indicates, in a very impressive manner, the vitality and richness that this art can contribute to the future visual environment of modern man.

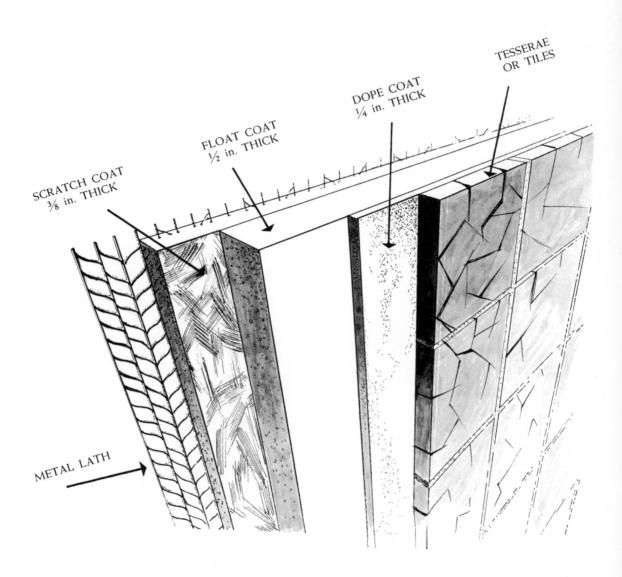

TESSERAE OR TILES

DOPE COAT ¼ in. THICK

FLOAT COAT ½ in. THICK

SCRATCH COAT ⅜ in. THICK

METAL LATH

One method followed by skilled tile setters for the installation of mosaic murals on walls. The tiles or tesserae are glued face down on a strong sheet of paper and are taken to the site and installed on the prepared cement wall.

Steps illustrating the preparation of a wall and the setting of mosaic using the reverse method. (Photos by Mosaicos Venecianos de Mexico, S. A.)

The metal lath surface of the bare wall may be used as is customary for tile-application roughing.

The bare wall is dampened and the scratch base trowelled in.

The scratch mortar base must be close
to plumb in true alignment.

A float coat is moderately trowelled
to a smooth surface.

The float coat must be kept wet to make trowelling easy.

True plumb must be constantly checked against guides and fixed plumb strings.

Mosaic sheets are "buttered" and applied over a surface and tamped into the cement.

After the sheets are set in cement the paper is dampened and removed by pulling downward.

When a tesserae pulls out, it is replaced after thoroughly cleaning the
spot.

Grout is applied next. A final cleaning
is done using muratic acid solution
and a wire or stiff bristle brush.

More and more, architects and designers are collaborating toward a reestablishment of the "team" effort in the creation of new edifices as worthy symbols of man's aspiration toward a sense of worthiness and beauty in a materialistic world.

Already, one observes, with fascination and delight in the squares and avenues of Europe and America, interesting attempts of mosaic murals on public buildings, schools, churches, store fronts, restaurant lobbies and interiors, and even in the lounges of ocean liners. A sort of uninteresting and mechanical surface and pattern may be seen at times, but this will come to pass when the real mosaicist, steeped in his art and sensitive to the potential and limitation of his media, will again infuse those little cubes of glass and marble with life and beauty.

Installation of P.S. 28 Auditorium Lobby Mural. Jack Stewart, who designed and made the mural, insisted on setting and cementing it on the wall. The bottom section of the mural has been tapped in place and the paper peeled off. The upper left corner shows the scratch and float coats of cement ready to receive another section of the mural which Mr. Stewart is preparing on the floor. Later the entire mural was grouted and washed.

Byzantine smalti mosaic mural, designed, executed, and installed by Jack Stewart, 1959, Auditorium Corridor, Public School 28, Manhattan (155th Street & Amsterdam Ave.), 5 x 7 feet. (Maurice Courland & Son, Architects—Nahama Courland, Interior Designer.)

At the site, the mural sections are set
into the wet cement beginning at the
bottom and right and moving upward
and to the left. As the cement is
beginning to set and harden, the brown
paper is peeled off by wetting it with
a sponge. The grouting process follows and finally a mixture of acid and
water is used for a washing.

Tools of Education, *a mosaic mural by Max Spivak for P.S. 189, Queens, Flushing. The mural measures 10 x 20 feet and was done in smalti. Mr. Spivak designed the floor, also in mosaic. (Michael Rodoslovich, New York City Schools, Architect.)*

Detail of a mosaic mural by Max
Spivak for the Cerebral Palsy School,
P.S. 48 of Staten Island, New York.
The mural, symbolic of the natural
world, consists of six panels and re-
ceived the Architectural League Prize.
(Michael Radoslovich, Architect.)

Large mural designed by Max Spivak of New York for the Charles Pfizer Company, Groton, Connecticut. Mural is 7½ x 32 feet and is made of smalti tesserae set in cement by the reverse method. The theme is WONDERS OF THE WORLD. The sun can be seen at the right, with fossils, earth structure, and vegetation right below. The sea, mountains, sky, solar system, man, and the atom to the right. (Screve, Lamb and Harmon, Architects.)

Detail of the Pfizer mural by Max Spivak showing man and the importance and development of antibiotics.

Religious mosaic mural, St. Peters Church, Pittsburgh, Pennsylvania. Made of smalti and set on the wall by the reverse method. (Rambusch Decorating Company.)

Mosaic mural, The Forum Of The Twelve Caesars Restaurant, Rockefeller Center, New York. (William Pahlmann Associates, Inc., Interior Designers, Executed by Rambusch Decorating Company.)

Ceramic mosaic mural for the Molbar Building in Beverly Hills, California designed by Architect C. Jay Parson. Random pattern and colors used. (The Mosaic Tile Company.)

Mosaic mural for the Edwards Restaurant, Skokie, Illinois, designed and executed by Salvatore Aucello. The mural is 8 x 10 feet. The various sections were set in place in a wooden framing. The ceramic tiles were glazed especially for this work by Mr. Aucello in his own kilns.

HOTEL SYMBOLS, *a mural designed and executed by Salvatore Aucello for the Kohler Hotel, Rochester, Minnesota, 5 x 35 feet. Special glazes and jeweled inserts were developed by Mr. Aucello for this mural.*

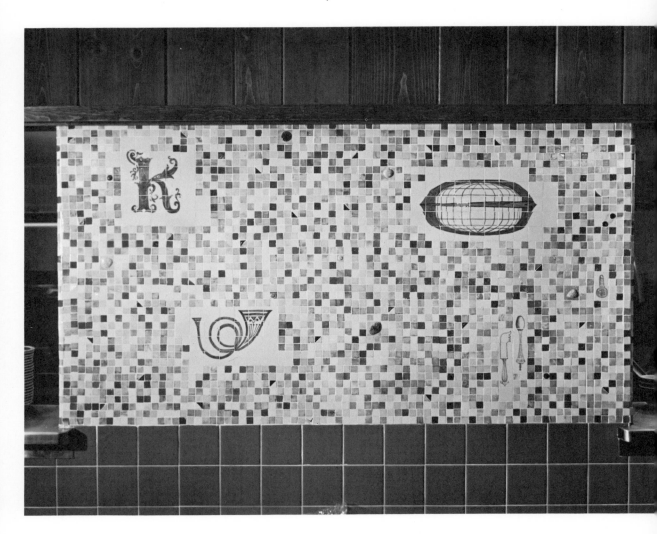

Venetian glass mosaic mural for the Bear Road Elementary School. North Syracuse, New York, by Edward C. Fricke. (Sargent, Webster, Cranshaw and Folley, Architects.)

Mural by Samuel G. Wiener, Jr. installed at the entrance of the Marjorie Lyons Playhouse, Centenary College. Mosaic was made of smalti tesserae and affixed on a brick wall.

Section of a mosaic floor designed by Samuel Wiener, Jr. using standard 2 x 2 inch unglazed tile, smashed, and applied directly with mastic.

MOSAICS FOR THE HOME

Exterior Uses

One of the most interesting developments in the revival of mosaics has been its application to the home.

The use of mosaics in the home of today has taken a dual approach. We observe new and interesting mosaics, including three-dimensional forms, used with utility and decoration as surfaces for outdoor wall plaques, terrace floors, swimming pools, and garden planters. This outdoor use of mosaics is particularly evident on the West Coast. Mosaics made their way into the interior of the modern home as articles of use and décor, also.

In recent years, Americans have reflected a new awareness of their natural surroundings. People like to entertain and spend their leisure moments outdoors. The terrace is a must, and much effort goes into its construction but little into its design.

A truly beautiful floor made of Venetian glass tiles and cement is a permanent and comfortable addition to pleasant outdoor living. The durability and color inherent in mosaics make the design and construction of outdoor table tops very desirable. Usually made of tiles set in cement in metal frames, these tables are serviceable and decorative.

The construction of a mosaic floor for a terrace begins with making of single slabs which may vary from 6 x 8 inches to whatever size one can handle efficiently. First a wooden frame is made and either nailed or notched together. Then heavy paper is placed underneath the frame. Mosaic tiles, Venetian glass in this case, are set in place at random with school paste.

A mortar of 1 part cement, 4 parts sand, and water is mixed and poured over the tiles.

Wall designs of mosaic tiles embedded in cement have been successfully designed for outdoor settings. Sculptures formed of brick and cement, and reinforced with a core of iron and covered with tesserae, have resulted in exciting pieces. Intriguing three-dimensional forms have been developed by arranging and composing with field stones and setting them permanently with epoxy adhesives. When completed, these mosaic-sculptures offer interesting opportunities for integration with plants outdoors. Another application of mosaic art outdoors is the construction of bird baths, water pools, and underwater sculptures.

The mortar is poured up to the edge of the frame and allowed to set overnight.

After the cement has set hard, the frame is removed and the slab turned over. The paper is "peeled" off carefully. Bits of glass which may pull out should be reset and allowed to dry.

The slabs, when thoroughly dry, are washed with clean water and a sponge or brush to bring out the colors and remove deposits of paste. Slabs should be stored indoors and covered with damp clothes or papers and allowed to dry slowly.

When enough slabs have been made, they are set on a "bed" of sand or cinders from 4 to 7 inches deep. A ½ inch space is left between slabs. These spaces are filled with a thin mixture of mortar.

A delightful garden floor designed and
executed by Jeanne Reynal. These
words are seen around the border: —
"I see a field of hands. When the sun
will shine these hands will open."

Interesting mosaic sculptures result from a design made with field rocks and stones, and with small pieces of smalti. Both stones and tesserae were set with epoxy-type adhesive and are ideal as garden decorations.

A piece of clay drain tile was transformed into a container by the application of pieces of Venetian glass in simple geometric patterns. Casein-type glue is recommended for indoors and epoxy-resin type adhesive for outdoors. A metal container was inserted inside. By Maybelle Coburn.

Interiors

Mosaics can be integrated in home accessories and décor very success-fully. They may be used as bases for table lamps, wall designs, fireplace facings, coffee-table tops, bar tops, jewelry boxes, ashtrays, and platters. They may find their way into the kitchen as counter tops, splashboards, window sills, and dinette or breakfast-table tops.

Many areas of a home can be brightened and made more cheerful by a mosaic which most people can make themselves. These objects are elegant, when designed in good taste, and practically impervious to accidents such as scratches and stains.

When used with sensitivity, the brilliant colors and everlasting quality of mosaic will add utility, elegance, and new life to a home.

Decorative wall hanging by John Kidder and James Dorris. Made with ¼ inch and ⅛ inch pieces of Venetian glass, using the direct method. (Mosaic Crafts of New York.)

Sensitive wall plaque by Pearl E. Ross.
Ceramic tiles were broken in random
pieces and set on plywood backing.
Design was grouted in white and
framed with walnut edging.

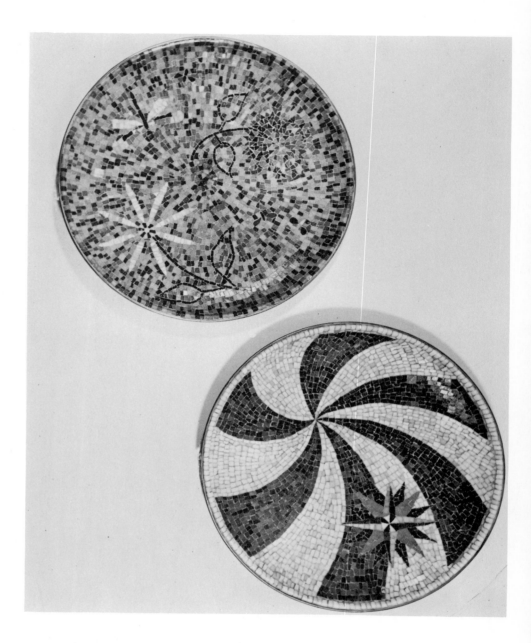

Two delightful platters made with pieces of Venetian glass set on a metal base with rubber-base adhesive and grouted. A platter can be hung on a wall as a decorative device or placed on a table for an arrangement to serve as a container. (Mosaic Crafts of New York.)

 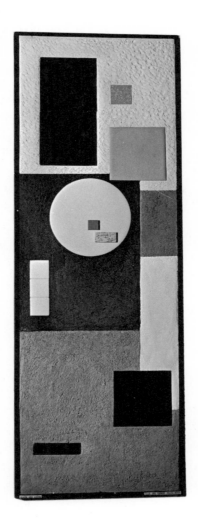

A mosaic wall design (left) by Pearl
E. Ross uses a frame of redwood to
contain vari-colored Venetian glass
tiles. An interesting wall plaque (right)
is made with a background of tex-
tured stucco with large and small ceramic tiles set for contrast.

Detailed view of a round table made
with flat beach stones and pebbles by
Robert Freimark. (The Davis Press,
Inc.)

Low table made with beach pebbles by Robert Freimark. Pebbles were set in cement and polished with paste wax to bring out the natural color of the stones. Mr. Freimark recently wrote in School Arts *that, ". . . Anyone creative is stimulated constantly to incorporate some of these resources into lasting enjoyment — to apply the beautiful mementos of nature to function. This is one way we beautify our daily lives." (The Davis Press, Inc.)*

Hexagon shaped low table of walnut
framing and mottled glazed tiles,
grouted in white. (Luberto of New
York.)

Low coffee table, 58 x 20 inches, made with domestic ceramic tiles in white, warm yellow, and black and then grouted. Top by Larry Argiro and legs by Nicholas Argiro.

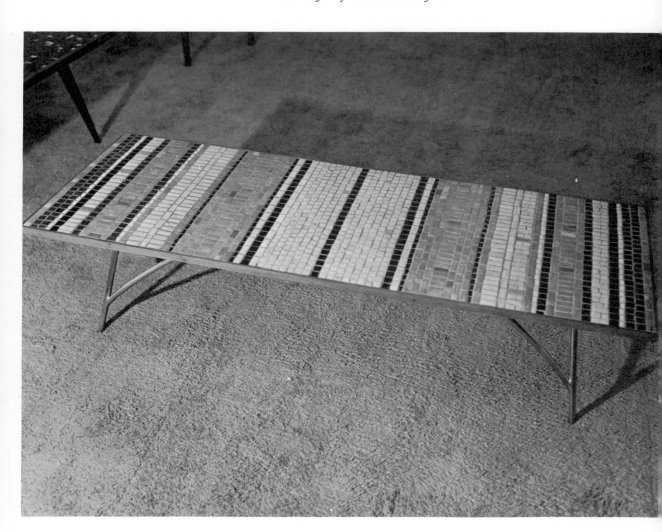

High side-table made of ceramic tiles broken at random. It has brass edging and walnut legs and is grouted for smoothness. Designed by Nicholas Argiro.

Teakwood and clay planting table, by Krevolin and Constantine, 20 x 50 x 14 inches, with two "double" planters set into the top, mosaic inlay of tan, gray, yellow, tiles (CRAFT HORIZONS.)

Round coffee table made with specially glazed tiles in off-white and golden brown, edging in brass and tile and legs in brass. (Mosaic Crafts of New York.)

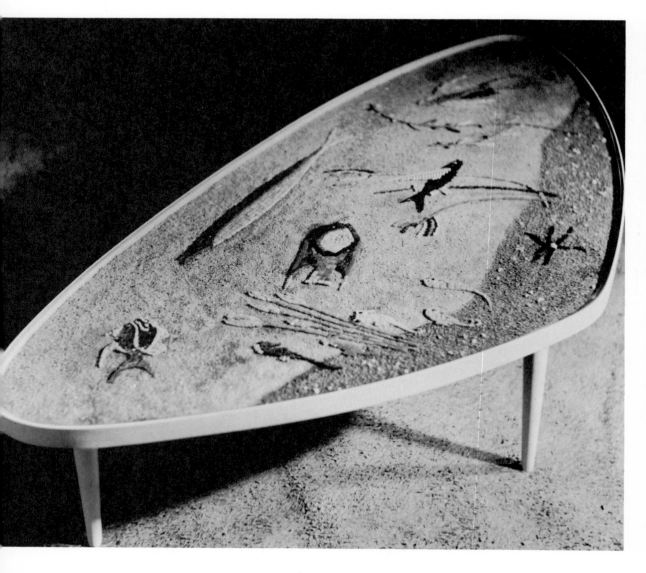

An unusual approach to the design of
a table top by Nicholas Argiro. A
three-dimensional effect was created,
suggesting under-water life, by building the mosaic with varied thickness
of glass, including granulated enamel.
A plate glass was placed on top to
provide a smooth surface and to act
as a window to the mosaic underneath.

Small round side table made of ceramic tiles fired and glazed in irregular shapes and set in cement and grouted white. The edging and legs are walnut. (Luberto of New York.)

Table lamp made of smalti tesserae in blue and blue-greens with accents of red and gold on a wooden frame. The base frame and legs are brass. Designed by Larry and Nicholas Argiro.

A low mosaic table, 48 inches in diameter, made with Venetian glass tessera ¾ inch square split to fit design, and "buttered" into place so as to give a sensation of radiation. Gold accents give the table a sparkling effect. By Larry and Nicholas Argiro. (Photo by William Howland and HOUSE BEAUTIFUL.)

Coffee table, designed by Vladimir
Kagan of Kagan-Dreyfuss, Inc., seems
to glow with luminous color. Made
with smalti tesserae in black, purple,
royal-blue, red, orange and yellow
with accents of gold, it has a frame
of walnut. (Photo by William Howland and HOUSE BEAUTIFUL.)

Several possibilities for the making of table lamps are suggested by various materials. Plywood bases and round cylinders (discarded rug supports) of heavy cardboard are covered with tiles and grouted. Electrical fixtures and shades complete lamps.

Kitchen splashboard is made permanent and colorful by setting ceramic
tiles with adhesive and later grouting.
Masonite board was used as backing
and pencil lines were drawn on it to
aid in positioning the tiles.

View of splashboard after it was grouted and cleaned. Yellow and white mottled tiles were used for background with accents of light and dark green. By Lucy Argiro.

Sheets of Japanese porcelain tiles are being set on a part of an old grand piano with casein glue by Lucy Argiro. These tiles are ⅜ inch square and are available glued face up on a sheet of mesh. Strips of sections of the sheet can be cut with scissors for setting on surfaces.

The table top is being grouted by spreading white cement with the hands. When split Venetian glass or ceramic tiles are being grouted, it is recommended to use a piece of cardboard so as to prevent cuts to the hands. After crevices are filled with white cement, the surplus is wiped off and the top allowed to dry.

The new table top is now ready for use. A silicone solution was applied to prevent the white grout cement from absorbing coffee or other stains.

*Countertop covered with ceramic tiles
¾ inch square. Tiles are Chinese red
with mottled edges in black. An "all-
over" pattern is used.*

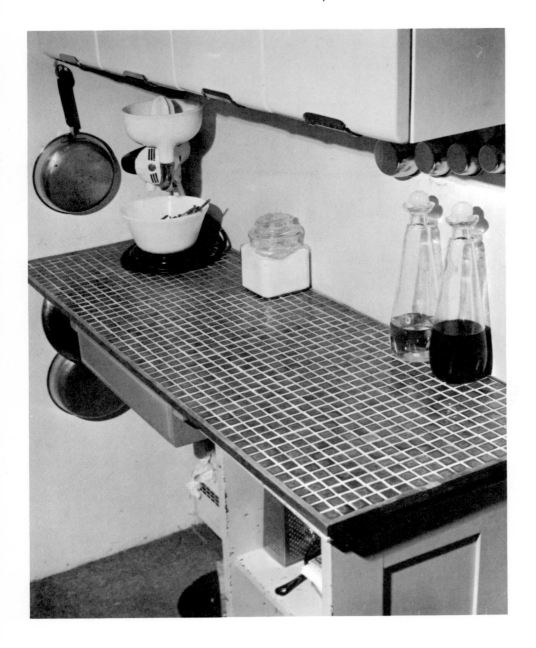

Application of mosaic on a windowsill.

An earthenware planter with rows of tiles.

Ordinary metal book-holders are made into mosaic book-ends by gluing a piece of masonite on the metal and covering it with pieces of Venetian glass cut at random.

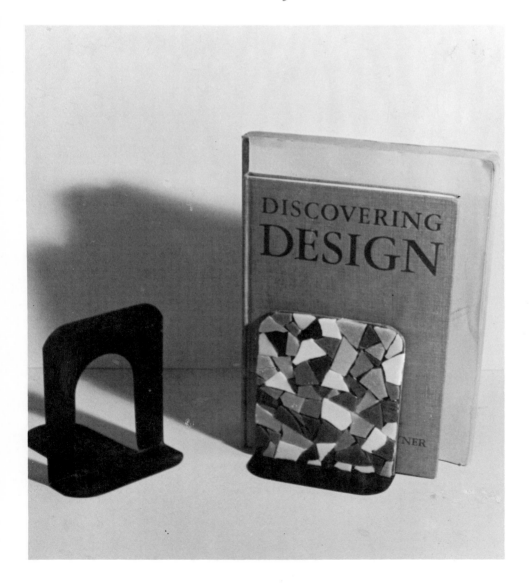

Bookends made with smalti tesserae in
greens with touches of black and gold
set on a solid piece of wood. The sides
are of polished brass.

VI MOSAICS FOR THE STUDENT

An important factor in the revival of mosaics has been its appeal to students. ·The term student is meant to include all those individuals who have a sincere desire to learn and to improve themselves.

This term student includes those individuals who are under formal teaching situations at different levels, the hobbyists who seek art activities as a form of recreation, and as amateurs or dilettanti those people who participate in art activities because they "love" or "find delight" in doing.

The continuing attitude of passiveness and tolerance toward the so-called hobbyist and amateur, and the implication that these individuals are good collectors of things and ideas but poor risks as innovators and regenerators, should be shelved.

A new look and a different approach is needed. The art educator should realize the great untapped potential of millions of people who openly demonstrate their need for and interest in art activities by purchasing countless prefabricated and spurious design devices in the mistaken idea that they are doing "art."

Thousands of amateurs today attend classes in mosaic design. Some are guided by inept individuals whose main interest is the sale of materials. Others are fortunate enough to meet such rare teachers as Sister Magdalen Mary at the Immaculate Heart of Los Angeles, and a truly creative art experience develops.

Paper mosaic by student.

The individual in public school or college is also fortunate that so many art teachers today have become interested in mosaics. At many schools this art is now being taught with competence at all levels.

Papier-mâché mosaic by Bernard Barnes.

Paper mosaic by Audrey Moss.

Paper mosaic by Jack Connolly.

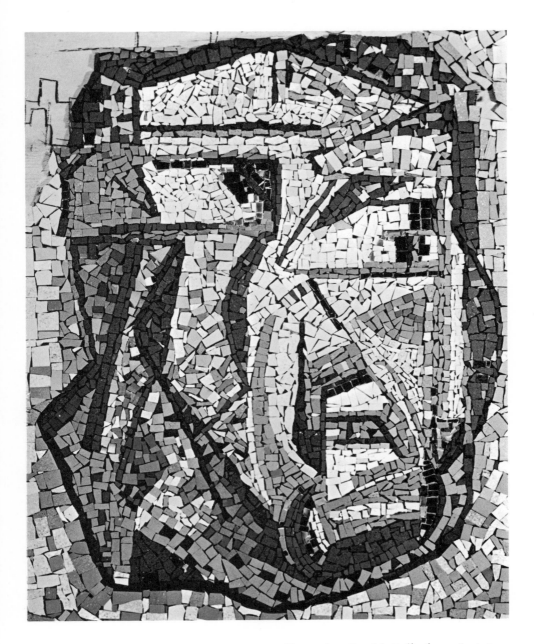

HEAD, by *Gerald Gallagher. An interesting mosaic created with very small pieces of unglazed tile, cemented to a wood panel with mastic. No grout was applied to this design.*

The cheerful, radiant, and firm personality of Sister Magdalen Mary has helped lift mosaic teaching from the doldrums of predesigned owls and breadboards to new heights and freshness in mosaic design in which the figure is used with dignity of style and seriousness of purpose. The works created by children and adults under the supervision of this energetic and busy Sister have been seen and admired throughout the country.

One is well aware of the currently accepted and practiced philosophy of art education. Its aims and goals have been firmly established by such recognized leaders as Victor D'Amico, Viktor Lowenfeld, and Italo de Francesco in their widely circulated books. These principles are given further guidance and implementation by Kenneth Winebrenner and *School Arts* magazine, by the National Committee on Art Education, and by the National Art Education Association and its related organizations.

Mosaic made with glass and brass by student of Professor Edward Fricke, Syracuse University.

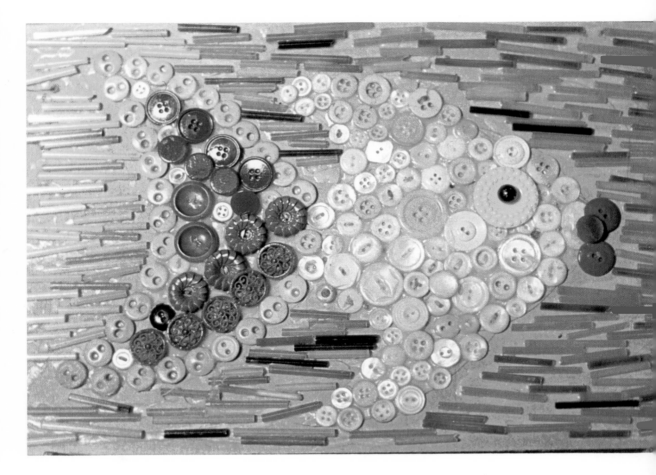

Mosaic made with plastic pieces by student.

Still, a few words on the teaching of mosaic art may be in order.

Mosaics have certain characteristics: animation of surfaces, reflected light, directional movement, texture, and color are the most important. A mosaic is a success or failure to the extent that these characteristics, and the intensification of some, are present in a particular work.

Inspirations for design ideas are everywhere. The natural world is an endless reservoir with its rock formations, clusters of leaves, accumulations of stones and pebbles, textures on tree-barks, and foam patterns on water in motion. Often neglected but always bursting with suggestions and inspirations is the myriad of activity found under a microscope, where a world of magic is revealed.

And the human drama provides other inspirations. What man does in his endless quest for self-fullfillment, his anguish and pain, his joy and delight, his excitement and frustrations, and his moments of relaxation and tranquility are sources of design ideas. The unique interpretation of events in history — both religious and social — provide countless suggestions. Inspirations are found in reading and understanding a poem, the sound of music, and the world of imagination. The natural and man-made environment and countless materials are constant inspirations for design ideas.

Someone once spoke of ". . . the discovery of the sensation of discovery. . . ." The translation of these words into a teaching-learning situation could immeasurably affect the results of people's efforts in art. First, the discovery that the very nature of the materials for the making of mosaics precludes fine and sometime superfluous detail. Second, the discovery that a direct and bold gesture will result in fresh and powerful visual images. And finally, the discovery that an attitude of planned carelessness, a state of mind which has been divested of the many blocs and obstacles erected by environmental patterns, will contribute greatly to the process of expression through materials of those elements within the individual which need expressing through a sense of form.

water currents and movement

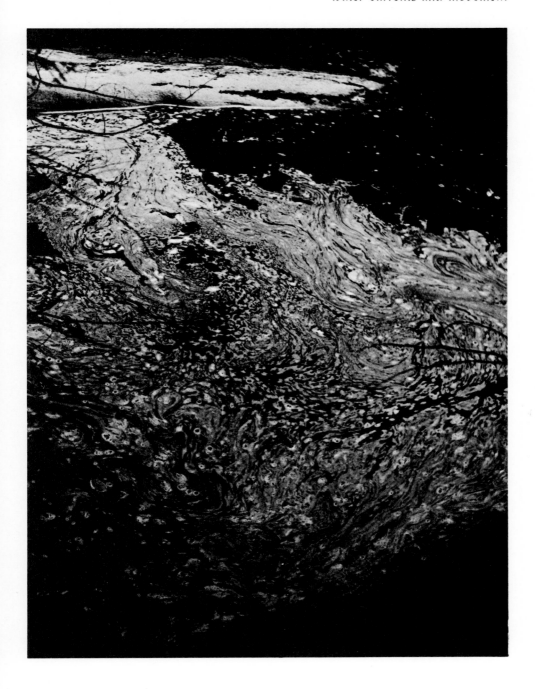

. lichens on a rock

effects of drought on soil and stones.

texture of a tree-bark

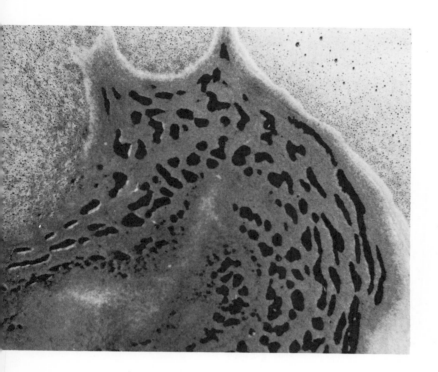

water, foam, and movement

pattern made of water and suds

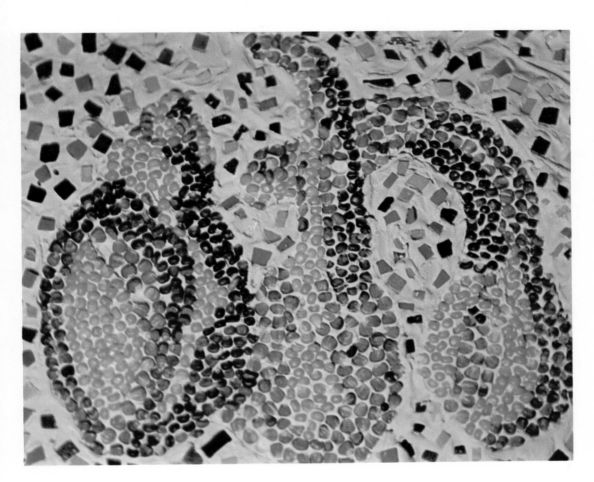

Mosaic made with seeds and glass by Bruce Cohen on background of cement.

Mosaic made with seeds and slate by
Nicholas Tedesco.

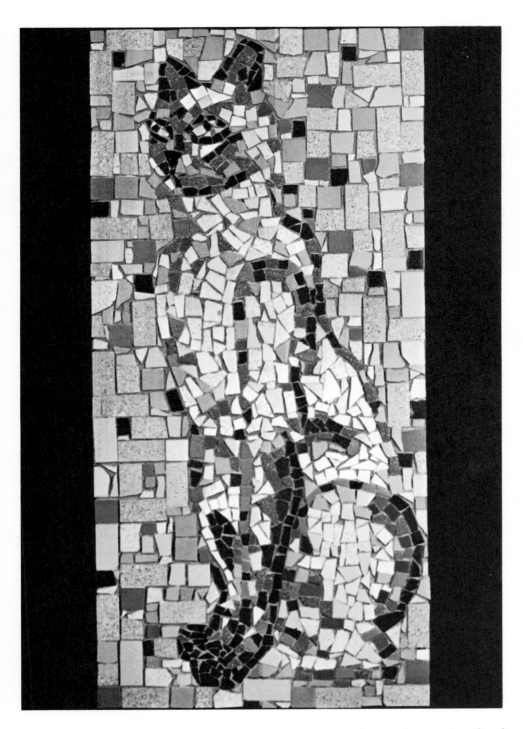

CAT, by Barbara Okvist. A stylized
design made with unglazed ceramic
tiles set with casein-type glue on a
wooden support and grouted with
tinted cement.

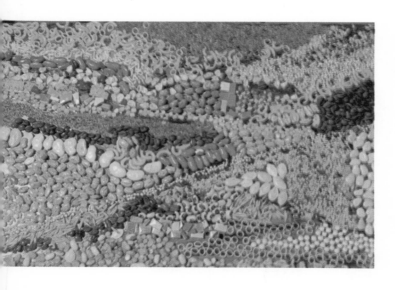

Mosaic with seeds and cereals by Herbert Din.

Abstract composition by Joan Terra-lavoro. Fragments of mother-of-pearl shells, reclaimed in a nearby button factory, were embedded in a layer of white cement (center), and granulated tesserae were sprinkled and pressed into masses of black mastic.

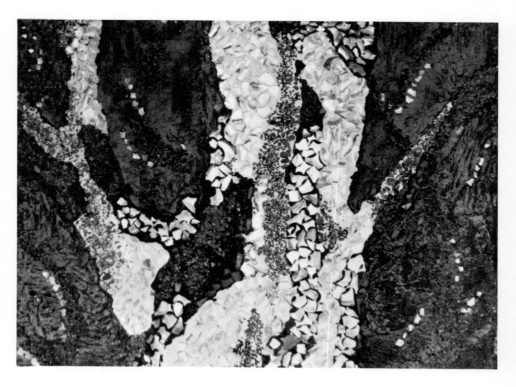

THE CREATURE, by Ruth Hinton, 25 x 40 inches. Venetian glass and smalti were used for most of this composition. Large areas are from slabs of melted coke bottles. Sister Magdalen Mary, I.H.M., Instructor.

TREES, *by Joan Terralavoro.*
Made with "marmi," small cubes
of marble. Background was lac-
quered and sprinkled with sand.

NATIVITY, *by Velma Bartholomew, 25*
x 37 inches. Made with ¾ inch Vene-
tian glass, around the edges, smaller
pieces embedded in cement and stained
glass in center background. Sister
Magdalen Mary, J.H.M., Instructor.

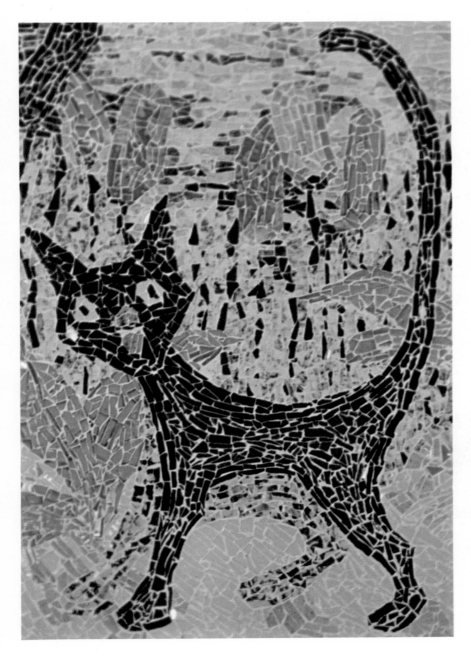

Ceramic mosaic by Dorothy Helm.

SUN AND TREES, by *Ann Milora*. Random pieces of granitex, a type of
unglazed tile, were arranged in a cir-
cular pattern. Warm hues, very
intense at the center, radiate outward
interwoven by dark outlines of trees.
Tiles were set flat-side with Elmer's
Glue-All on a plywood panel.

MOTHER AND CHILD, by *Elizabeth Shay. This semi-abstract impression was realized by splitting granitex tiles into irregular pieces and setting them on the narrow side. This gives the mosaic a palpitating feeling. The halos were suggested by pressing small gold spheres in cement.*

COMPOSITION, by *Milo Dalby. Fragments of rocks and shells were combined to achieve great textural effects
and movement in this mosaic. Sand
and carborundum powder, sprinkled
on the still wet cement, helped give
unity and contrast to the mosaic.*

CITY AT NIGHT, by *Bruce Cohen. An
impressionistic fresco-mosaic made
with joint system cement mixed with
pigments. Very small bits of Venetian
glass and granulated enamel were
spread and pressed into the wet
cement.*

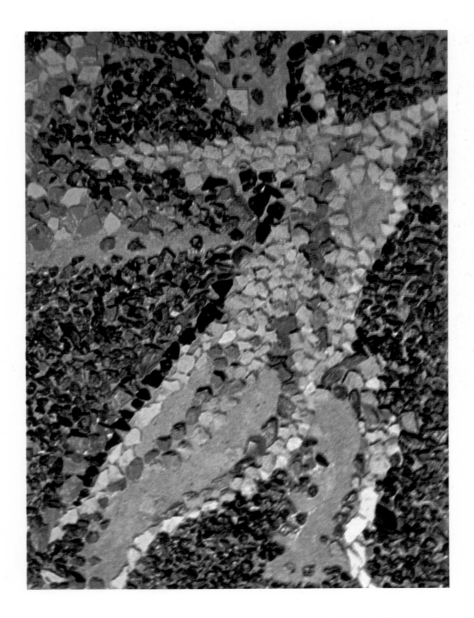

Mosaic made with crushed stone by Milo Dalby.

COMPOSITION, by Pearl E. Ross. This mosaic is an interesting use of pebbles. White and brown pebbles were pressed in an impasto of mastic which had been tinted with green oxide. A few fragments of red enamel were embedded between the pebbles for accent.

CRAB, by Pearl E. Ross. The background was made with light cement. Black pigment was added for the center form. Pieces of glass and ceramic tiles were pressed in the wet cement.

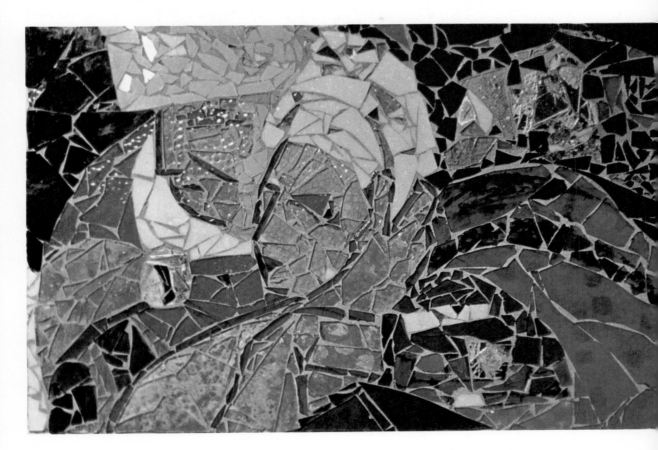

Mosaic design made with stained glass remnants. Glued on plywood panel and grouted. By John McHugh, High School of Art and Design, New York City.

Mosaic made with stained glass as found at random. Crevices are filled with clear lacquer and sprinkled with carborundum black dust.

An "active" and interesting mosaic by Pola Yolles. It was made by pressing shells in grey mastic and surrounding them with pieces of ceramic tiles.

TREE, by Michael Passaic. Different types of wood veneers were cut in irregular pieces and glued on a plywood panel. The wood mosaic was finished by spraying two coats of clear lacquer on the surface. A casein-type glue was used.

These examples of student's work in mosaics have been selected because of the diversity of materials and techniques used and for the promise they suggest for extended opportunities in the future.

Some of these mosaics were created by students majoring in art education, some were made by elementary teachers at in-service training classes, some are the efforts of children, and few are by amateurs. This was the first experience in mosaics for many of them. All work in this chapter was done by the author's students unless otherwise stated.

Random pattern mosaic background was used by Ottavio Manco for his copper repousse' made in the sculpture class of Professor Ben Karp.

Tin containers transformed into ash-trays by applying ceramic tiles with Ply-bond and by grouting.

This unusual wall hanging was made by Georgia Wilson with smalti and enamel tesserae and a casein-type adhesive to a support of mahogany adapted from a discarded grand piano.

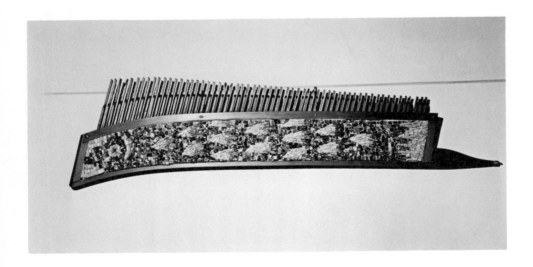

Bisque ceramic bowl and saucer made into mosaics.

Two mosaic designs made by students of the State Art Institute of Venice, Italy. "Marmi," marble, tesserae were used and set in white cement on a backing of pressed fibres. (Courtesy Professor Mario Pellarin.)

MADONNA AND CHILD, by *Alice Leonard. A mosaic sculpture built on a framework of chicken wire and papier mâché. Melted bottle glass and pieces of stained glass were pressed in a layer of mortar about 2 inches thick. Sister Magdalen Mary, I.H.M., Instructor.*

A geometric composition by Georgia Dunn. Made with Venetian glass, it was grouted with black cement for the light areas and white cement for the black ones.

A wall design by Myra Stillman, housewife-writer. This is her first attempt at mosaic-making. Glazed ceramic tiles were used directly on plywood panel. The bottom area was painted and built up with sprinkled sand.

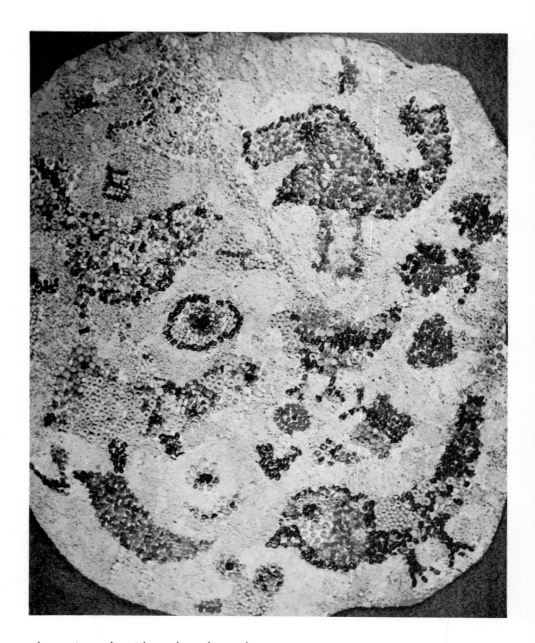

A mosaic made with seeds and cereals by children of the Decatur Public Schools. Design is free and spontaneous. (Photo by Edith Brockway. The Davis Press, Inc.)

Mosaic design made with glass marbles. The marbles were split in half on a "hardy" and set in a layer of gesso.

Simple hot plate and bowls.

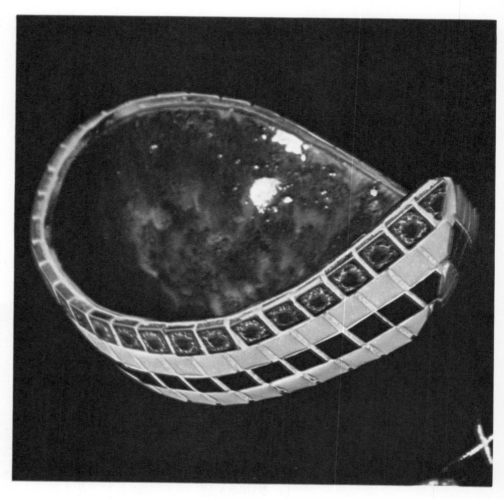

Bowl with ceramic tile decoration.

Another example of sand casting and mosaics. Shell fragments were pressed in the wet sand before plaster-of-Paris was poured. Relief by Audrey Aguglia.

Venetian glass and glass marble were used in this sand casting. Tiles and marble were pressed in the moist sand mould just before white cement was poured. This experiment is by the author.

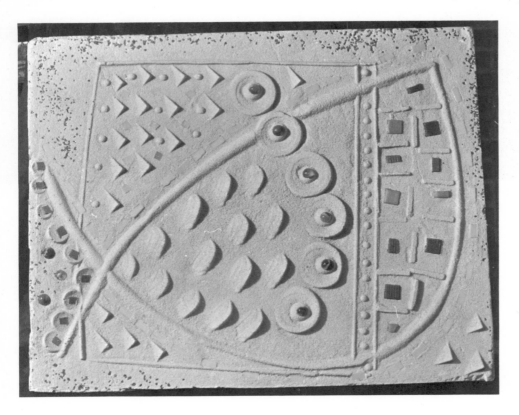

Jewelry box made of walnut and
topped with Venetian glass.

A wall plaque, in relief, designed by
Ottavio Manco. Background tiles were
set flat-side and grouted. The tiles on
the relief were set on the narrow side
and left ungrouted.

Mosaic of cereals and seeds by Donald McClure.

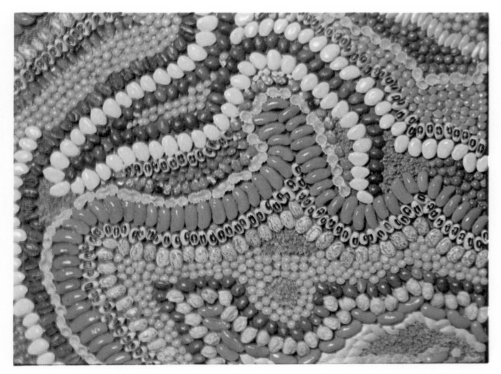

Mosaic made with seeds by Sarah Flynn.

Mosaic made with seeds by Rita Gottlieb.

VII MATERIALS FOR MOSAICS

Commercial Materials

Real mosaics, as traditionally produced from Roman days on, consist of four types. These are the marble or "marmi," enamels or "smalti," Venetian glass, and ceramic tiles.

Corner of studio of Elsa Schmid. Containers with quantities of "smalti" and parts of enamel pancakes from which smaller tesserae are made.

rubber and vinyl tiles   marble   wood

cork tiles   shell fragments   stained glass   seeds

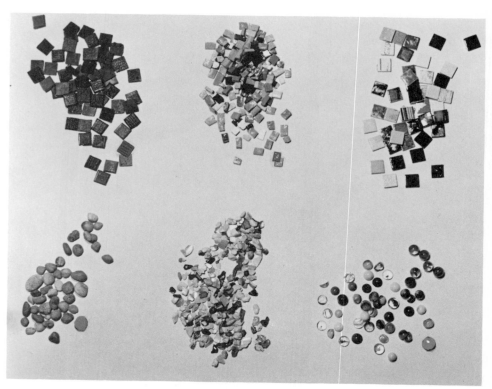

Top row, from left: ¾ inch Venetian glass tiles; smalti tesserae, also called Byzantine glass or enamel; and ceramic tiles.

Bottom row, from left: beach pebbles; aquarium bits of shells, and glass marbles.

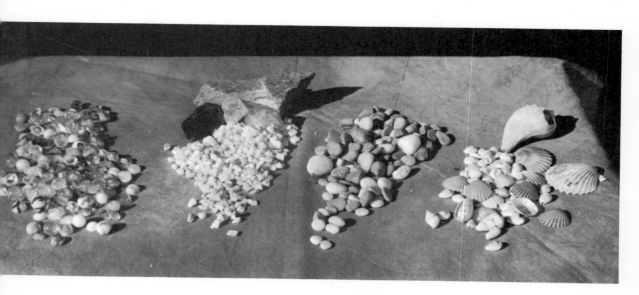

glass marbles   crushed rock   beach pebbles   shells

Marble or "marmi." Small cubes of various colored marble found in the marble quarries of Europe. The large blocks of marble are first sliced into one-half inch thick slabs, using special saws and running water. These thin slabs of marble are then cut into smaller pieces and finally chopped into almost perfect cubes.

This hand chopping process was recently observed in a mosaic shop in Ravenna, reminiscent of exactly the same procedure used by tessera cutters 1600 years ago and earlier.

Marble tessera, used almost exclusively up to the 4th century, is now available and can be identified by some interesting names. Yellow Siena, Botticino Beige, Rosa Corallo, Bardiglio Grey, Belgium Black, Green Isogne, Rosso Verona, and Yellow Mori are some of the most popular colors. Prices range from $.60 per pound for white to $.92 for most other colors. Yellow Siena sells for $1.00. These one-half inch cubes are a bit too thick for some work and they may be cut into halves, thus obtaining double coverage from a given number of cubes.

Tessera being split on a "hardy," a special cutting device used for centuries by mosaicists. It is still preferred by most professionals today.

A new type of "hardy" designed by the author. A Stanley brick chisel has been inserted in the center of a heavy wooden block. The cutting hammer was made from a Stanley brick hammer by shortening and sharpening the ends.

A different type of "hardy" made from a piece of angle-iron which was hardened. A modified Stanley brick hammer is used as a cutting hammer. When a regular "hardy" is difficult to obtain, one of the variations can be easily made.

A pair of tile-nippers, available in
most hardware stores, will split most
tiles. The Gundlach tile cutter No. 85
C and the Starrett adjustable jaw cut
nippers with tungsten carbide tipped
jaws No. 1X were found most satisfactory for continuous use with all
types of tiles.

Enamels or "smalti." The oldest and most beautiful are the small and irregular cubes of enamel, sometimes called Byzantine glass. Because these small chunks of enamel are cut by hand from a larger "pancake," usually produced in Venice, they are rather irregular in size, shape, and surface. This characteristic has made the "smalti" a favorite with artists throughout the ages. These roughly rectangular pieces of opaque glass enamel are vibrant and light-reflective. Their size is about $\frac{1}{4}$ by $\frac{3}{8}$ by $\frac{1}{2}$ inches and they range in price from $2.00 to $6.00 per pound and it takes about $2\frac{1}{2}$ pounds to cover one square foot of space.

Venetian glass. These tiles are made of glass, marble dust, and pigments. The mixture is high-fired to a lava-like consistency, after which it is poured into metal molds not unlike a waffle iron. When cool, the tiles are removed from the molds and pasted face down in rows of 15 on a square foot of paper. Made primarily for commercial purposes, these mosaic glass tiles are three-quarter inch square and one-eighth inch thick. They can easily be cut into halves or quarters with a good pair of nippers. Because the surface is very smooth, these tiles are excellent for table tops, fireplaces, counter tops, trays, bowls, and wall plaques. They are impervious to liquids and are scratch proof. Each square foot contains 225 tiles; prices range from $1.20 to $4.00 per square foot for the reds and persimmons, and $8.00 for the gold and silver.

Ceramic tiles. This type of tile is very popular with the beginner because it is easily cut into any shape or size with a simple pair of nippers or a pair of cutting pliers. Ceramic tile is made of clay and has a thin coating of glass on the surface. Colors vary from solids to fancy and mottled shadings, including gold. Because ceramic tiles are porous, they are not recommended for outdoor use, especially where the climate is severe. They are excellent for picture making, trays, tops of any kind, counter surfaces, walls, lamps, bookends, and any object for the home and office. These tiles are usually three-quarter inch square and one-eighth inch thick and are made in Italy, in Puerto Rico, and, in large sizes, in the United States. Prices range from $.70 per square foot for most solid colors to $2.35 for the red-gold mottled. They can be obtained with a high gloss or a mat finish.

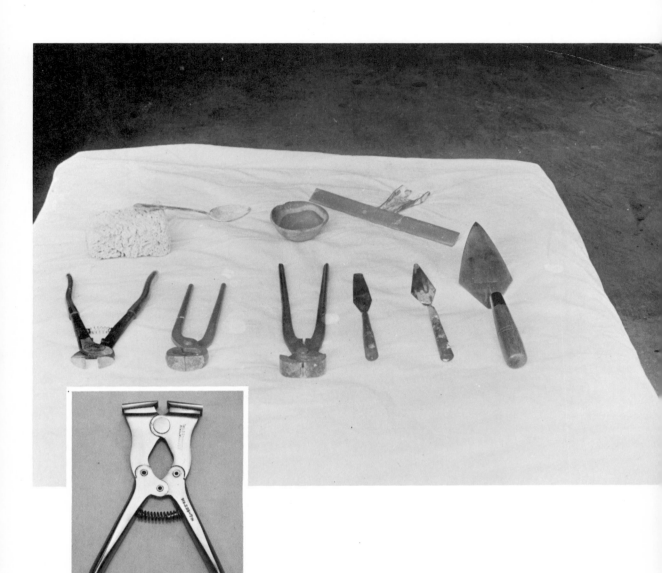

Some basic tools needed for work in mosaics. Shown are various types of tile-cutters, spatulas for mixing, sponge for cleaning, and squeegee for spreading cement when grouting.

smalti   *Venetian glass*   *ceramic tiles*   *unglazed tiles*

Porcelain tiles. A new tile, recently imported from Japan, is being used with increasing success in schools and adult centers. This tile is small, three-eighths inch square and one-sixteenth inch thick, cuts easily to any desired shape, and has a very smooth, even surface. The tiles are highly fired and the glazes used on the surface are very glossy.

Unglazed ceramic tiles. These tiles are made in many of our tile manufacturing centers and are available in several sizes. Made for commercial use, when these tiles are cut into smaller pieces, they make excellent material for wall plaques, table tops, and other accessories.

Other Materials

Although commercially produced mosaic tiles are most favored by the professional mosaicist, other materials have been used with success. This is especially true when an experimental attitude is involved and local school budgets do not allow for expensive items. Many of the materials suggested here can be found in any area of the country or can be purchased at reasonable prices.

Pebbles and beach stones. A diverse variety of small pebbles are to be found almost everywhere. River banks and beaches provide fine sources for the accumulation of pebbles with unusual shapes and colors. Gravel deposits also contain small stones which can be adapted to mosaic work. Both pebbles and stones should be washed before being glued permanently on a mosaic panel. This cleaning process will bring out more vividly the subtle tones and colors in the stones; a spray or coating of clear lacquer or plastic will preserve the colors indefinitely.

Glass marbles. These colorful spheres of glass are similar to Venetian glass tiles. Some show an intriguing inner core of liquidlike streaks of color. These round marbles can be used intact, or they can be split in half for more effective adhesion. Glass marbles are most effective when used in conjunction with other materials.

Paper and cardboard. Mosaics can be made with ordinary paper from colored magazine advertisement pages. Commercial colored poster and construction papers can be used, but these lack the surface finish of the coated papers. Mirrorlike paper in solid colors, sold by art supply dealers, lends itself to interesting designs. Metallic papers and foils are particularly useful as accents or for special effects.

Shells. Unusual mosaics can be made by using various shells or segments of shells found on most beaches. The corrugated surfaces and subtle color of these shells provide the means for imaginative and delicate mosaics. A spray of lacquer or plastic will help bring out and retain the color of these shells.

Stained glass. This material offers many possibilities. The practical consideration of flatness is combined with a unique depth of color resulting from the transparency of the glass. Irregularly cut pieces of stained glass are sold by weight, and prices vary according to location. Firms who make stained glass windows will supply small quantities of remnants of assorted colored glass.

Broken glass. Bottles, in a wide range of colors, can be broken into small pieces and glued on a flat glass pane, or embedded in cement or plaster of Paris. These broken pieces catch and reflect light with sparkling results and are particularly effective where a nonobjective mosaic is desired. This material is not recommended for use with children.

Sharp edges of broken bottles can be eliminated by "tumbling" them in a ball mill. Fragments of glass are placed in a jar or container holding balls, pebbles, or carborundum powder and water. The jar is rotated on a tumbling machine and the grinding action eliminates the sharpness of the edges in a few hours. Another method used to produce slabs of glass is to melt broken bottles. Pieces of jagged glass are arranged on shelves and melted in a pottery kiln. Concave fragments of bottles flatten out in the fire and the edges become round and smooth.

Broken china. Remnants of broken dishes can be broken into smaller pieces and used for a variety of mosaic designs. Because both the top and bottom of these pieces are smooth and even, they can be used for the flat surface needed on such articles as trivets, table tops, and wall plaques. A local pottery may be a rich source for this material.

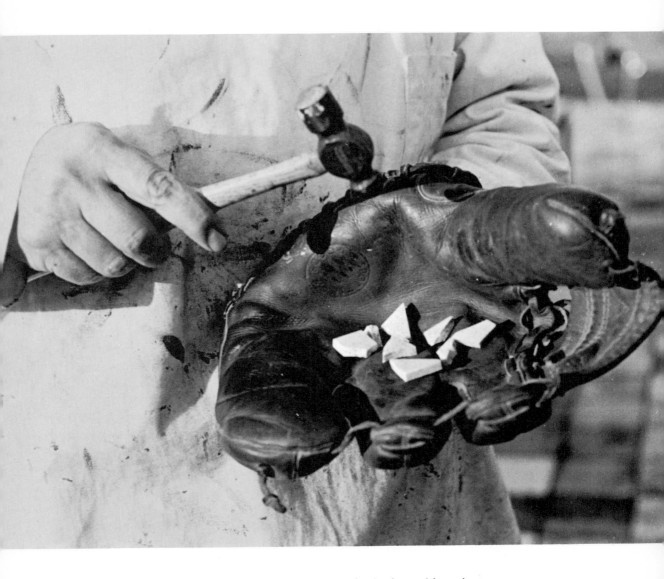

One method of quickly splitting random pieces of unglazed tiles or other large pieces of flat material. Old baseball glove protects hand from injury. The Ball-peen hammer is good for striking tiles, but other types work as well.

Plastics. Plastic wall tiles have been cut into small squares and used effectively. Any piece of plastic of reasonable thickness can be cut with shears or a saw. Because the edges of this material are not very sharp, it can be used safely at any grade level. Plastic factories dispose of a great amount of defective pieces of plastic in sheet form or in the form of manufactured objects. Such plastic is very valuable in the creative hands of children in the classroom.

Linoleum. This material is reasonable in price, easy to cut into small pieces, and fun to work with. One rubber tile used for flooring, when cut into one-half inch square pieces, will make a great amount of smaller tiles. Floor covering stores will sell at reasonable prices a wide assortment of linoleum remnants in a variety of colors. A good pair of shears is sufficient for cutting this material. Vinyl and other synthetic floor covering, including cork tiles, should be considered for experimental purposes.

Seeds. Seeds offer an endless source of interesting material. The many seeds vary in size, shape, color, and texture. Lima beans, yelloweye beans, northern white beans, peas, corn, rice, pumpkin and mellon seeds, wildbird seeds — these and many others challenge the imagination.

Cereals. Extruded forms of cereals and macaroni that are found in a grocery store offer delightful possibilities for the very young mosaicist.

Minerals and rocks. The locality in which one lives will, in a sense, define or limit the use of minerals and rocks. But the possibilities offered by such unusual shapes, colors, and textures as found in quartz, lava, crystals, calcite, flourite, copper ore carbonate, asurite, malacite, and others open vast and exciting new horizons. Larger pieces can be broken down to the desired size with a hammer. These pieces are most effective when used along with other materials.

Assorted materials. The number and variety of man-made and natural materials that can be used for the making of mosaics is vast indeed. Depending on the type of design, age of the designer, and scope of the art activity, one can suggest an almost unlimited supply of materials which can be found in the basement, closet, attic, shop, or department

This operation shows the cutting of tiles in quantities. A special electric saw, equipped with a diamond-tipped blade and a continuous spray of water, will cut glass, ceramic, and unglazed tiles in any width. An entire strip of tiles can be cut in moments.

store. Large and small buttons of unusual shape, color, or design are effective when used with discrimination and sensitivity. Imitation pearls, jewels, and sequins can add just the right touch and sparkle to a mosaic design. Broken pieces of mirrored glass, silver or gold coated, have great possibilities, along with bits of such metals as brass, copper, and aluminum. However, one must be cautioned against the careless use of these materials lest an unhappy conglomeration of assorted pieces results.

A tumbling machine can be used to smooth and round the sharp edges of broken glass. A container is filled with pieces of broken bottles, carborundum, or sand and water and is placed on the two rubber-covered shafts.

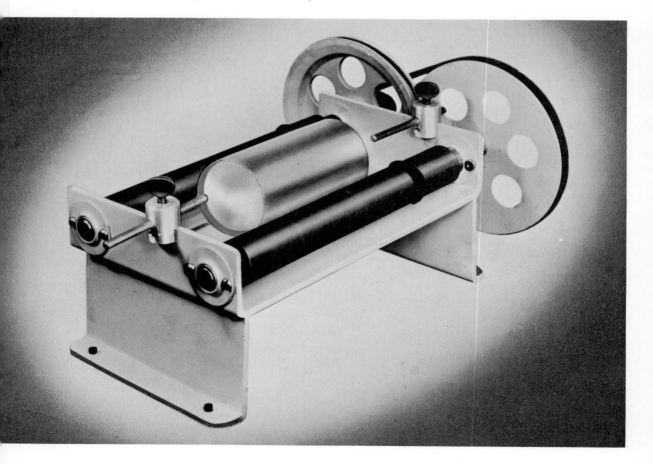

VIII PREPARING TO MAKE MOSAICS

Backing and Supports

After a design for a mosaic has been created and the materials selected, consideration must be given to the type of backing or support which will hold them together.

Ordinary gray chipboard or mounting board is good for paper mosaic designs, but when using other materials, such as shells, seeds, stone, and glass, more rigid backings are required. Heavier cardboards will be sufficient in some cases, but pressed board material, such as Masonite, is recommended. Masonite boards are available in various thicknesses and the larger the design the thicker the board must be. Rigid Masonite one-quarter inch thick will support a panel up to six feet square.

Such pressed boards as Homosote and Celotex are adequate for the beginner, but because of the soft core of these boards they are not recommended for panels larger than two or three feet square unless. reinforced with wooden or metal framing. The rough and fibrous surfaces of these boards make them ideal for good adhesion; smooth boards should be scored or roughed up a bit.

Plyscord, an unfinished building grade of plywood, will result in stiffer and more permanent panels. Sheets of Plyscord are similar to sheets of regular plywood, except that the surfaces are unfinished. Actually, the roughness of the surface of Plyscord is better suited for effective adhesion and its price much lower than plywood. It is advisable to strengthen larger panels of Plyscord by fastening diagonal bracing on the backs. Another fine backing material is Novoply. This composition board is very strong and warp resistant.

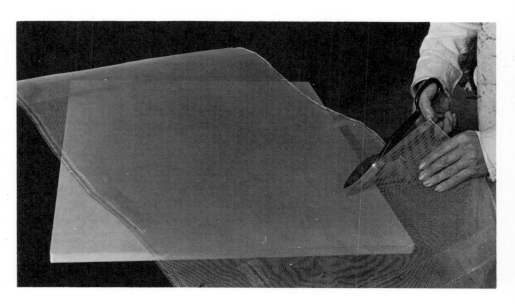

A good backing for a mosaic can be made from plywood panels. To insure better bonding, a sheet of wire mesh or screening is fastened to the panel with carpet tacks. This procedure is recommended when using as background a paste-like mixture such as cement or magnesite. The wire mesh is not necessary when using flat tiles such as Venetian glass or ceramic tiles. Any of the casein-type glues will work well on smooth surfaces.

A backing for a coffee table made of a 5-ply plywood panel. The walnut frame, ⅛ inch veneer, was superimposed on the backing. The frame should be masked with tape and heavy paper to protect it from scratches and moisture when the finished surface is grouted.

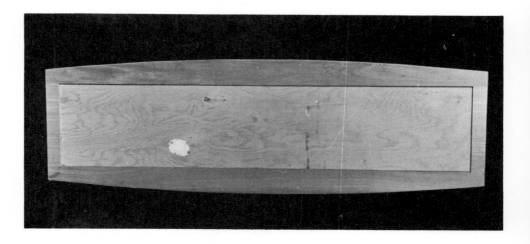

Lumber distributors often have in stock slightly damaged hollow-core door panel which can be purchased at a reduced price. The lightness and strength of these panels makes them fine for backings of large wall designs. They are available in sizes ranging up to 36 inches in width and 7 feet in length, and are often used as backings for mosaic coffee and dining tables.

Most of the casein-base white glues are best suited for these flat surfaces. If a cement-type adhesive must be used, it is recommended that a screen mesh be nailed on the smooth surface of the panel with small carpet nails or tacks. The cement will be impregnated through the mesh and thus produce a better bond. This will prevent the finished mosaic from peeling off the backing when the cement dries. As a substitute for the wire mesh, a coat of glue can be spread on the smooth surface before the cement is spread on the surface.

A really rigid and permanent backing is achieved with angle-iron framing and expanded metal sheets. This type of backing is successful when using mortar cement or magnesite as background and base. The angle iron, one-half inch for small panels and one inch for larger ones, is mitred at the joints and bent into the desired size and shape. The ends may be welded, brazed, or bolted together. A sheet of expanded metal is then cut to fit within the frame made by the angle iron, and the sheet is dropped into place. Lastly, both frame and sheet are bolted or welded together. A rigid and strong backing results, especially for outdoor mosaic designs.

The cement impasto is troweled directly onto the sheet, up to the edge of the frame, and the tiles are pressed directly into place. Newspaper should be spread underneath the backing before troweling begins.

Plate glass or double-strength glass panels make excellent backings when a transparent or light-producing mosaic is being designed. Most of the clear-drying casein or acrylic glues can be spread thinly on the surface of the glass panels, and then the stained glass, Venetian glass, or "smalti" tesserae pressed into place. A frame, housing adequate light tubes, should be constructed. The finished panel should be inserted in precut grooves in the frame. A very interesting colored illumination of a mosaic

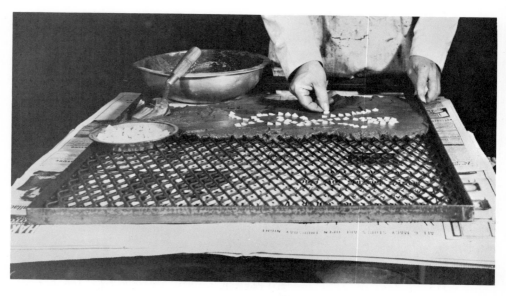

This support for cement or magnesite based mosaics can be used outdoors as well as indoors. A sheet of expanded metal is inserted in the angle iron frame and is either bolted or welded into place. The cement mixture is spread on the metal grid and the tesserae is pressed into place. Newspaper should be placed under the panel to prevent cement from adhering to the table or bench.

A brass edging was fastened to a round plywood base in making a support for a beach-pebble mosaic table for use on a terrace. Wire mesh was fitted and nailed to wood and brass inserts are part of the design.

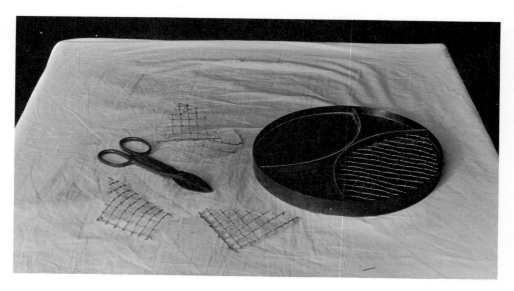

will result. If necessary and desired, sheets of Lucite or Plexiglas can be substituted for glass.

Cements and Grouting

Grouting is the technique of filling the crevices between tesserae with a mixture of thin cement. This is necessary to obtain a smooth surface for coffee-table tops, working surfaces, counter tops, trays, and trivets, or as weatherproofing for some outdoor murals and some wall designs, depending on the function and effect the mosaicist is trying to achieve. Weatherproofing of some mosaics, especially when ceramic tiles and Venetian glass squares have been used, prevents moisture from seeping into the mosaics, and in case of frost, eliminates cracking and peeling of tesserae.

Interesting supports for three-dimensional mosaics can be made by experimenting with field stone and rocks. These were arranged and set in place with epoxy-type glue. Areas to be joined together should be cleaned. Tesserae can be set on rocks with the same adhesive. Appropriate pigment can be mixed with the glue so that it will blend with the stone.

Other sources for support of a three-dimensional nature are made by joining together pieces of clay drain-pipes.

Three-dimensional supports for sculpture mosaics can be designed and built with cement mortar on a structure of twisted wire mesh. A rough surface should be left on the form (scratch coat) on which to spread the final layer of cement for the direct setting of tessera.

Mosaics are usually grouted with a mixture made from a very fine white cement. The cement itself is at times referred to as grout. It is sold in 25-pound bags and costs about $.25 per pound. Marble dust or fine white sand is sometimes mixed with the white cement. This adds to the strength of the mix and eliminates the possibility of shrinkage.

More common cements, such as either gray or white ordinary Portland cement, have been used for grouting with success. All of these cements can be tinted by mixing dry mineral pigments with the dry cement before adding water.

The three-dimensional structure partly covered with mosaic tiles. Sculpture was unfinished when photograph was taken.

In making mosaics with seeds, pebbles, shells, pearls, or marbles, grouting is not only unnecessary but may actually cause damage to the materials.

Framing

Most mosaics require no framing. This is especially true of wall panels. However, table tops and some panels seem to function better within a frame.

A one-eighth inch wood stripping is recommended for framing. Woods frequently used are walnut, mahogany, and birch. A natural finish is obtained by applying two coats of clear lacquer and a final rubbing with wax.

Pine stripping one-eighth to one-quarter inch thick can be attractive when painted with a black satin enamel or lacquer and gold leaf applied on the top side. This procedure helps make a lovely frame.

Brass stripping is available in various sizes and must be attached with brass tacks or screws. For lasting beauty, the brass stripping should be polished and cleaned, and a final spray of clear lacquer applied. This is not necessary when the stripping has been lacquered during manufacture.

Three-dimensional wall plaques can be made with a support of thicknesses of wood arranged and nailed in place. The tesserae are set in place with appropriate glues or cements, depending on the exposure and use.

Good supports or backings for trays or platters can be made from discarded materials. Shown are some of the types of supports, especially made for mosaics on the left, and round concave disks of various sizes, on the right. Resin-type glues are spread after the surfaces have been thoroughly cleaned, and the tiles are then set in place. Some of the large disks are made with a hook welded on the back for use as wall hangings.

Attractive and useful bookends can be made from supports of wood as shown. Sides of the book-end can be finished with brass or veneer edging.

WAYS OF
MAKING MOSAICS

This chapter has been written especially for the classroom teacher, the art instructor, the student, and the amateur.

Materials used by the very young for making mosaics should be of the type that need no cutting or splitting. When the young child is using colored paper, he can be encouraged to use his fingers to tear larger pieces into smaller ones for the mosaic design he is creating.

It is generally agreed that for the elementary school child, few or no tools are required except what can be found in an average classroom, such as scissors, paste, mucilage, and cardboard. This understanding is very important at the beginning of this discussion, since it should be made clear to the classroom teacher and art teacher that they need no elaborate tools and supplies for carrying on art activities through mosaics.

The following presentation deals with problems which a beginner faces when he involves himself in the making of mosaics with hard and permanent materials.

Cutting and Splitting

Ceramic mosaic tiles can be cut or split with ease when using a pair of ordinary cutting pliers. The teeth of the pliers should grasp no more than one-eighth inch of the tile; if a little pressure is applied at the end of the handles, the tool will cut right through the tile. Moving the tile or pliers in any direction will make possible the cutting of any shape or angle.

Dr. and Mrs. Carl Werts of Los
Angeles and their six children are
enthusiastic students of mosaics. They
came under the influence of Sister
Magdalen Mary and, with her as a
teacher, created some noteworthy
mosaics. They are shown putting the
final touches to a religious panel made
on a plywood board using ceramic
and unglazed tiles "buttered" directly
in place.

A young student at Arlington Central School, New York working with paper to design a mosaic. Small paper tesserae are pasted on heavy cardboard.

Sister Magdalen Mary's students making the papier-mâché forms for mosaic sculptures. Chicken wire was used to help reinforce the large structures. One student is seen spreading a layer of cement while another is beginning to press glass tiles in place.

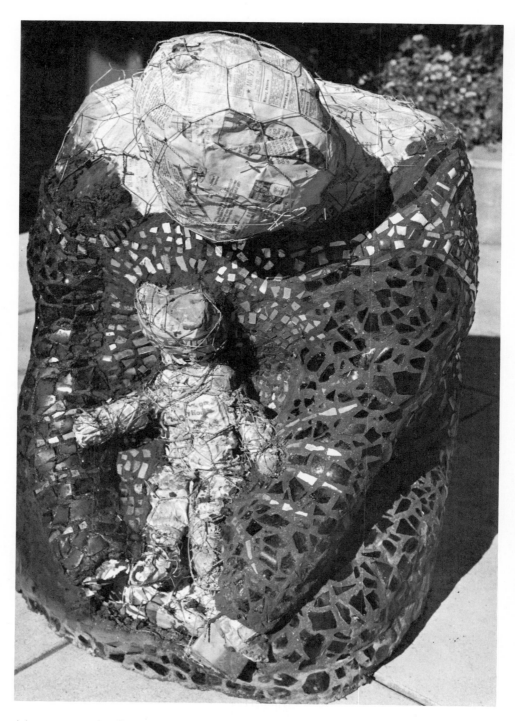

MADONNA AND CHILD, *partly com-
pleted, in the studios of Immaculate
Heart College of Los Angeles. Sister
Magdalen Mary, I.H.M., Instructor.*

MADONNA AND CHILD, *the completed mosaic sculpture by Joan Gabriel. Immaculate Heart College, Sister Magdalen Mary, J.H.M., Instructor.*

Venetian glass mosaic tesserae are more difficult to cut, but the process can be made rather simple when a good pair of tile-cutting nippers is used. This tool cuts a clean and accurate line across the tile. Further cutting of the tile into smaller sizes and shapes is very simple.

One side of the tile, glass or ceramic, should be inserted one-eighth inch into the jaws of the nippers. The nippers or the tile should be moved about in any desired direction for parallel or diagonal cuts. The application of some pressure at the end of the nipper handles will cause the tile to split right through. Very accurate cutting will be possible after some practice.

Thousands of glass tiles have been cut without injury, but it is recommended that ordinary safety glasses or plastic shields be worn by the student during the process of cutting.

One will find in working with these materials that some tiles which contain very little marble dust are more difficult to cut and apt to splinter. This is true of black, red, copper, and some gold and silver tiles.

Adequate tile-cutting nippers can be purchased at most hardware stores. These range in price from $.90 to $15.00, and the type selected will depend on the amount of work to be done and the type and thickness of the tiles to be cut. A good pair of nippers can be purchased for about $2.00 and can be used for both ceramic and glass tiles.

Some of the nippers that have proven satisfactory are Gundlack, Red Devil, Utica Tools, Channellock, Goldblatt, and others. The Starrett Company makes a carboloid-tipped cutter which the professional seems to prefer because its machinelike action assures accurate cutting with a minimum of pressure.

Some professionals split "smalti" and "marmi" tesserae on a *hardie*. A hardie is a wedge shaped piece of steel which has been secured firmly on a solid base such as a tree trunk.

A junior high student arranging and setting a mosaic made from fragments of fired clay. Student of Bernard Barnes, Newburgh Public Schools, Newburgh, New York.

Working with cereals and seeds, children of the Decatur, Illinois elementary schools make interesting mosaic designs. Mastic is spread on masonite board and materials pressed in. (Photo by Edith Brockway. The Davis Press, Inc.)

At left, a layer of joint system cement was spread on a backing of Celotex. Top shows dark hued tesserae embedded upright in the cement. Bottom section shows unglazed tile embedded flat-side in cement. The right section shows the same procedure as on the left except the cement was mixed with black pigment to help accent contrast of lighter hued tesserae. Experiments like these are suggested for developing various types of grounds and textures.

Author's student, Deanna Blankfine, is shown splitting unglazed tiles, granitex, with Gundlach nipper and cementing them up-right on a plywood panel. The surface has been "scored" or roughed up with sharp instruments for better adhesion of joint-system cement.

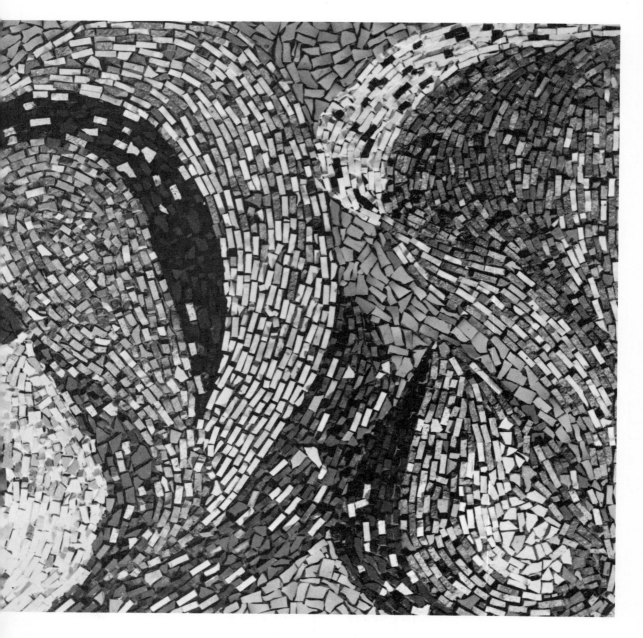

Finished mosaic design using irregular pieces of granitex, a type of unglazed tile, by Deanna Blankfine.

Detail of Deanna Blankfine's mosaic showing interesting directional movement and rhythm of tesserae. Some pieces were set up-right and others flat-side. Unusual textural qualities were developed.

Adhesives and Glues

The specific material to be used must determine the particular type of adhesive selected. The location of the mosaic, outdoor or indoor, also determines the selection of adhesives.

The paste or mucilage usually found in most classrooms and art departments will suffice for the making of paper mosaics. Mucilage or any of the casein-based glues can be used when working with seeds, cereals, and similar materials.

For more permanent work, to be kept indoors, it has been found that Elmer's Glue-all, made by Borden Company, is satisfactory. This adhesive is easy to use, dries clear, and keeps well in its plastic container. Other fine adhesives are Sure-Bond, Pioneer Latex, Rivet, Armstrong, and Willhold. Miracle Black Magic, 3-M, Ply-Bond, and Bond-Master are rubber base adhesives and are recommended for advanced work and, under certain conditions, for outdoor exposures. The last two adhesives work satisfactorily on metals.

One of the epoxy resins, a truly remarkable bonding material, is ideal for difficult bonding problems. This material is expensive, but worth having for some special work. It is sold in two separate containers, one containing the epoxy resin and the other the catalyst or hardening agent. Small tubes are sold for about $.89, but larger quantities can be purchased in quarts or gallons. As with most other adhesives, the original bonding agent, clear or white, can be tinted to desired tones by the addition of mineral oxides.

Cements and Magnesites

A very good adhesive can be made from a mixture of the type of cement called *joint-system cement*, which is used by plasterers for filling joints in dry wall construction.

Joint-system cement should be mixed by adding the powder to clean, warm water and stirring until the powder is completely wet. The mixture should be stirred again after a 30 minute wait. The cement will then be ready for application to the backing. The desired consistency

MOTHER AND CHILD, by the author, detail showing the animated pattern achieved when using pieces of unglazed granitex tiles, broken at random in an old baseball glove, and set flat-side, directly on plyscore backing with Elmer's Glue-All. Outline accents were made with thin pieces of black tile split with Gundlach tile nippers. The surface was grouted with tinted cement, most of which was wiped from crevices to create deeper shadows around each piece of tile.

Unusual textural surfaces can be created by using granulated mosaic chips, white sand, carborundum dust, sequins, rhinestones, gold and silver dust, marble chips, dry pigments, and other similar materials. The mosaic is designed with planned unfilled areas. The design shown is about finished; tesserae were set in defined spaces only. Empty areas were next painted with two coats of pigmented lacquer related to the selected color harmony.

of cement may be obtained by adding either water or powder. Dry mineral pigments (oxides) can be added to color the off-white cement for tonal backgrounds. This adhesive cement is excellent for the beginner. It is available almost everywhere, is relatively inexpensive, and is easy to prepare.

Next, a frame was nailed or fastened around the panel and painted areas were "flooded" with clear lacquer. Eye droppers or plastic containers with small tapered lips are useful containers for pouring lacquer. The selected granular material is sprinkled on the lacquer as it becomes "tackey." This is a basic procedure and further experimentation and variations are advised.

Rich and colorful textures are thus achieved in contrast to the mosaic areas. This design suggests an underwater impression.

The making of a mosaic tray or platter begins with the cleaning and sanding of the metal base with steel-wool, emery-cloth and scouring powder. Metal adhering glue, such as Ply-Bond, Bond-Master, 3-M and Black Magic, is spread on sections of the tray, starting on the outer edge or at the center and moving on to adjacent areas as the tesserae are set in place.

When all tesserae have been set in place, the platter is set aside and the glue is allowed to dry.

A batch of white or tinted cement is mixed in a container to cake-batter consistency and stirred thoroughly.

The mixed cement is poured on the
surface of the tesserae . . .

. . . and spread and pressed into all crevices between each tessera. The platter (table top, lamp base, or other surfaces) should be allowed to stand for about five minutes. The excess cement is then wiped off.

The final wash or cleaning is done after the cement has set for about ten hours. The surface is now scrubbed with sponges, wash cloths, paper towels, and if needed, scouring pads and steel wool. Venetian glass surfaces are more difficult to clean while surfaces made with ceramic tile clean easily.

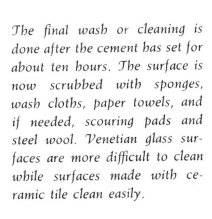

The grout or cement can be made water-proof and stain proof by applying a wash of liquid silicone to the surface of the mosaic. It may be necessary to repeat this application a few times in order to make certain that the cement is well impregnated with silicone.

A variation of a mosaic wall panel is one which transmits the full strength of color by the action of artificial light. A sheet of double-strength glass (18 x 24 inches) was used as a backing. The tesserae (Venetian glass) were split into irregular shapes and set to the glass sheet with Weldwood Presto-set glue. For experimental purposes, the glue was spread on one section of the glass and the tesserae set in place, leaving a clear space around the sheet for sliding it into the box.

In another section, each tessera was "buttered" and set in place. The design evolved intuitively as it progressed.

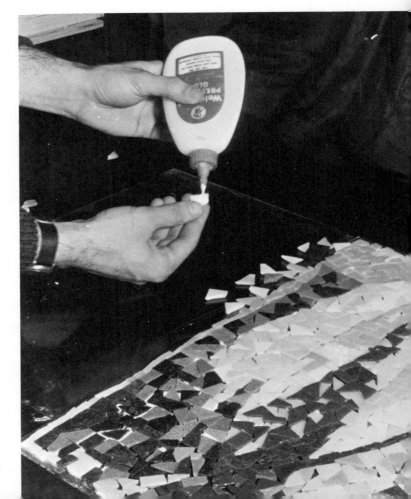

The "gesso" mixture, made by the American Art Clay Company, has been used with success on wooden backings for the adhesion of both glass and ceramic tesserae. It is highly recommended since it acts as both adhesive and grout. "Swedish putty" is similar, but is a bit stronger than cement and is very effective. It can also be tinted and will function as both an adhesive and a grout.

Magnesite cement is favored by some professional mosaicists. This product is more difficult to prepare, store, and purchase than many other cements, but it is stronger and can be modified for both indoor and outdoor mosaics.

Magnesite is a quick-setting cement which at times is used for the construction of flooring. It dries stonelike overnight and adheres well to wood and to any type of tessera.

Magnesite comes in powder form and must be mixed with a special liquid chemical made from chloride crystals. The strength of the cement can be controlled by adding more crystals to the liquid solution. The addition of fibres to the dry cement will also strengthen the mixture. Nylon or silk shreds and asbestos have proven to be good reinforcing materials.

Occasionally, fine or coarse sand is mixed with the powdered magnesite. Doing so tends to lessen shrinkage and warping. The basic color of magnesite, usually a light beige, can be changed by adding dry pigment to the powder before mixing it with the liquid chloride.

Magnesite is not sold in small quantities; one must purchase it in 100-pound bags. The chloride is also sold in large quantities in liquid and in crystal form. Most people prefer the liquid chloride because the crystals, when left in a sack, will "bleed" and dissolve on the floor. Large glass jars or containers should be used for storing both crystals and liquid. If metal containers are used, they will soon erode and thus are not recommended as containers for storage.

A special waterproof magnesite cement can be purchased in larger distributing centers and it can be used for mosaic panels which are to be hung in patios or gardens.

Next, a wooden box was constructed.
A groove was cut in the sides through
which the glass sheet was inserted.
Two electric sockets were wired and
fixed in place. A sheet of aluminum
foil was placed in the back of the box
for intensification of the light. One of
the short sides is removable. The box
is finished with dark stains or black
satin enamel.

After the glass panel is set and dry it
is inserted in the grooves. When the
light was turned on, strong and dis-
turbing sparks of clear light came
through where tesserae has been "buttered" on the glass. The glue had not
completely covered the surface. Sections which were covered by spreading the glue gave a more subtle and
even distribution of light.

Since prolonged work with magnesite with bare hands can be harmful, rubber gloves should be used when mixing a new batch of liquid or mortar. Parts of the human anatomy which are exposed for long periods to magnesite cement and chloride crystals should be washed frequently.

Application of adhesive can be made by "buttering" each piece of material or tessera and pressing it to the backing. This direct application is preferred by some who wish to follow, with care, the outline of a predetermined design on a backing.

A different manner of application is spreading the adhesive in a given area and setting each piece as fast as possible. Some adhesives dry rapidly and cause a "skin" on their surface, in which case care must be taken to break through this skin when pressing the tiles in place.

Useful tools for spreading adhesives or cements are small and large trowels, serrated spatulas, and palette knives.

LIGHT-MOSAIC, *by Bruce Cohen, as it looked when finished.*

GLOSSARY

Aesthetics. Strictly speaking, the theory of perception, but in a more exclusive sense, the science of the beautiful.

Alabaster. A somewhat half-transparent stone capable of high polish.

Buttering. A method of applying glue or cement to a tile with a palette knife.

Byzantine Art. The art which owes its origin to Byzantium (A.D. 328 to A.D. 1204).

Cartoon. A full size sketch made by artists preparatory to execution of murals. Derived from the paper used for this purpose which was called "cartone" in Italian.

Ceramic. The art of manufacturing objects or tiles made of clay and decorated with a thin layer of glass.

Enamel. A semiopaque vitrified material which is melted and applied to various metals. It is colored by mixing various metallic oxides.

Filato. A method of making miniature mosaics by using thin sticks of enamel. Derived from the Italian "filo," which means thread.

Fresco. A painting executed on a fresh ground—in Italian "al fresco"—of lime and gypsum.

Granitex. A type of unglazed tile normally used for flooring.

Grout. A thin mix of fine cement used to fill cracks. Also the process of using the cement to fill up or finish a tiled surface.

Hardy. A sharp tool with a double-beveled edge, used to split tesserae.

Intaglio. The process of decorating an object by depressing below the surface. The reverse of a relief.

Intarsia. Wood or marble cut and filled with similar materials or mosaic.

Joint System Cement. Strong bonding material used for filling joints when constructing dry walls.

Laminated Glass. Two thin layers of glass placed one over the other and fused together. Gold leaf is placed between the sheets of glass to produce gold tesserae.

Magnesite. A strong cement normally used for flooring but also applied as a base for mosaics.

Marmi. Small cubes of marble betwewen one-quarter and one-half inch thick.

Mastic. Some of the various cements or mortars used for setting tiles.

Matrix. A groove or cut in which gems or stones are set.

Mortar. A mixture of lime, sand, and water for setting or cementing bricks, stones, and tiles.

Mosaic. The process of putting together pieces of hard, colored substances to form a design.

Nipper. A type of plier with sharp jaws which will cut tiles or wire.

Oro. Italian for gold. Refers to tesserae made of gold leaf laminated in glass.

Oxides. Powdered chemicals used as agents to induce color.

Rout. To cut by scooping or gouging.

Silicone. A nonmetallic crystalline element used to waterproof porous materials such as cement.

Smalti. Small cubes of enamel, hand-cut from one-half inch thick pancake-like shapes. Also referred to as Byzantine tesserae. Italian for enamel.

Spackle. A hard-drying cement used to fill cracks and joints.

Stained Glass. Materials produced by fusing siliceous sand with certain alkaline earths or salts and metallic oxides.

Stucco. A fine plaster for walls or their relief ornaments, made of Portland cement, sand, and lime.

Tessera. A small cube or square of enamel, glass, or stone used in the making of mosaics. From Greek, meaning square piece.

BIBLIOGRAPHY

Design and Art Education

BEAN, PHILIP C. *The Language of Art*, New York: The Ronald Press Co., 1958.

DAMAZ, PAUL. *Art in European Architecture*, New York: Reinhold Publishing Corp., 1956.

D'AMICO, VICTOR E. *Creative Teaching in Art*, rev. ed., Scranton, Pa.: International Textbook Co., 1953.

DeFRANCESCO, ITALO L. *Art Education, Its Means and Ends*, New York: Harper & Brothers, 1958.

DOWNER, MARION. *Discovering Design*, New York: Lothrop, Lee & Shepard Co., Inc., 1947.

EMERSON, SYBIL. *Design: A Creative Approach*, Scranton, Pa.: International Textbook Co., 1953.

FORD, K. M., and CREIGHTON, T. H. *Design for Living*, New York: Reinhold Publishing Corp., 1955.

GRAVES, M. E. *Art of Color and Design*, New York: McGraw-Hill Book Co., Inc., 1951.

KAUFMANN, EDGAR. *What is Modern Design?*, New York: The Museum of Modern Art, 1950.

KEPES, GYORGY. *Language of Vision*, Chicago: Paul Theobald, 1949.

MOHOLY-NAGY, L. *Vision in Motion*, Chicago: Paul Theobald, 1947.

WICKISER, RALPH K. *An Introduction to Art Education*, Yonkers, N. Y.: World Book Co., 1957.

Mosaics

ANTHONY, EDGAR W. *A History of Mosaics*, Boston: Porter Sargent, Publisher, 1935.

BETTINI, SERGIO. *Mosaici Antichi di San Marco a Venezia*, Bergamo, Italy: Istituto Italiano D'Arti Grafiche.

BLANCHET, ADRIEN. *La Mosaique*, Paris: Payot, 1928.

Bovini, Giuseppe. *Ravenna Mosaics*, New York: New York Graphic Society, 1956.

Dalton, O. M. *East Christian Art*, Oxford: The Clarendon Press, 1925.

Furnival, W. J. *Leadless Decorative Tiles, Faience and Mosaics*, Staffordshire, England: W. J. Furnival, 1904.

Gentili, Gino Vinicio. *The Imperial Villa of Piazza Armerina*, Rome: Istituto Poligrafico dello Stato, 1956.

Graber, Andre. *Byzantine Painting*, New York: Skira International, 1953.

Huch, Ricarda. *Early Christian Mosaics*, New York: Oxford University Press, Inc., 1946.

King, Albert H. *Mosaic and Allied Techniques*, Los Angeles: Southern California W.P.A. Art Project, 1940.

Kitzinger, Ernest. *J Mosaici di Monreale*, Palermo, Italy: S. F. Flaccovio, Editore, 1960.

Lowrie, Walter. *Art in the Early Church*, New York: Pantheon Books, Inc., 1947.

Male, Emile. *Religious Art*, New York: Pantheon Books, Inc., 1949.

Meyer, Peter. *Byzantine Mosaics*, Batsford, England: Iris Colour Books, 1952.

Morey, C. R. *The Mosaics of Antioch*, New York: Longmans, Green & Co., Inc., 1938.

Mosaiques Byzantines, Athenaeum, Les Documents Photographiques, Paris: Editions Alpina.

Muratori, Santi. *J Mosaici Ravennati della Chiesa di S. Vitale*, Bergamo, Italy: Istituto Italiano D'Arti Grafiche, 1942.

Sherrill, Charles H. *Mosaics*, London: John Lane, The Bodley Head Lts., 1933.

Toesca, Pietro. *J Mosaici—La Cappella, Palatina di Palermo*, Milan, Italy: Edizione D'Arte Sidera, 1955.

Whittemore, Thomas. *The Mosaics of Hagia Sophia at Istanbul*, London: Oxford University Press.

Young, Joseph. *Course in Making Mosaics*, New York: Reinhold Publishing Corp., 1957.

LIST OF SUPPLIERS

Carrara Marble Company, 8653 E. Garvey Avenue, South San Gabriel, Calif.

Dillon Tile Company, 252 12th Street, San Francisco, Calif.

M. Flax Art Supplies, 10846 Lindbrook Drive, Los Angeles, Calif.

Leslie Art Supplies Company, 2220 W. 7th Street, Los Angeles, Calif.

Los Angeles Tile Jobbers, 3371 Glendale Boulevard, Los Angeles, Calif.

MacGregor-Sanders Associates, 1369 Laurel Avenue, San Carlos, Calif.

Mosaic Tile Company, 829 N. Highland Avenue, Hollywood 38, Calif.

Pomeroy Art Supply, 6412 Selma Street, Hollywood, Calif.

Eastern Tile and Marble Company, Miami, Florida.

Beno J. Gundlach Company, 11 N. 8th Street, Belleville, Ill. (Tile nippers.)

S. E. Rice and Associates, 7068 North Glenwood Avenue, Chicago, Ill.

Hatfield Color Shop, 161-163 Dartmouth Street, Boston, Mass.

The Starett Company, Atholl, Mass. (Tile cutters.)

Gager's Handicrafts, 1024 Nicollet Avenue, Minneapolis, Minn.

Casavan Carrara Marble Company, 1 Mount Vernon Street, Ridgefield, N. J.

Cermicraft, 6 Morris Turnpike, Summit, N. J.

Agency Tile Supply Company, 522 West 29th Street, New York 1, N. Y.

Albert Constantine and Son, 2050 Eastchester Road, New York 61, N. Y. (Wood veneers.)

Leo Popper and Sons, 143 Franklin Street, New York, N. Y.

Miya Company, 373 Park Avenue S., New York, N. Y. (Pebbles.)

Mosaic Crafts, 80 West 3rd Street, New York 12, N. Y.

Murals, Incorporated, 16 East 53rd Street, New York 22, N. Y.

Scharff Trading Corp., 414 East 75th Street, New York, N. Y.

F. E. Schundler Company, 28 41st Street, Long Island City, N. Y. (Magnesite.)

Speiden-Whitfield Company, 206 West 23rd Street, New York, N. Y. (Magnesite.)

Standard Tile Company, 854 Rockway Avenue, Brooklyn, N. Y.

Tile Distributors, Inc., 1112 East Tremont Avenue, New York 60, N. Y.

Otagiri, 222 5th Avenue, New York, N. Y. (Pebbles.)

Mosaic Tile Company, Zanesville, Ohio.

Immerman and Son, 1020 Euclid Avenue, Cleveland, Ohio.

F. E. Biegert Company, Inc., 4801 Lemmon Avenue, Dallas, Texas.

Ugo Dona, Murano, Venice, Italy.

Mosaicos Venecianos de Mexico, S. A., Cuernavaca, Mor. Mexico.

INDEX